GEO-MANIPURALERT

GEO-MANIPUR ALERT

Dr. R.K. Ranjan Singh
&
Ch. Debala Devi

AKANSHA PUBLISHING HOUSE
New Delhi • Guwahati • Visakhapatnam

AKANSHA PUBLISHING HOUSE
4649/21-B, Ansari Road
Daryaganj, New Delhi - 110 002
E-mail: ektabooks@yahoo.com
Phones: 011-23263193, 09435116718

Geo-Manipur Alert

First Published, 2010

ISBN 978-81-8370-170-9

PRINTED IN INDIA

Published by Akansha Publishing House, New Delhi - 2 and Printed at S.N. Printers, Delhi.

Dedicated

to

My Parents

Content

Acknowledgements

During the middle part of the December, 2004 I was thrown into extreme trouble and hospitalized for more than two months. My left leg was made deformed by a certain group of our own community demoralizing the whole approaches and efforts of the eco-movement in the State. I was under a severe mental tension. During this period of mental depression Shri Irengbam Arun (Editor: Ireipak), Shri Hanjabam Priyokumar Sharma (Desk Editor, AIR Imphal), Dr. M.C. Arun (Associate Professor of Anthropology, M.U.), Dr. L. Sarat (Retd. Selection Grade Lecturer, Manipur College) suggested me to publish a book collecting all the papers/ articles which were presented at different academic platforms and fora of International, Regional and National level workshops and seminars etc. Without their inspiration, I may neither prepare nor publish this book. The gestation period of this book has been a long one, with seven years of cocoonisation of the scripts by me and ultimately my wife Smt Ch. Debala Devi (co-author) took the initiative for drafting the final script. I would like to acknowledge the countless efforts and encouragement from/by various organizations and colleagues will remain ever encouraging during these seven years of academic devastation.

I would also like to thank Shri M.P. Misra, Akansha Publishing House, New Delhi, for the final outcome of this book.

Authors

Preface

Land and water are ecologically linked into systems called catchments or watersheds. From the smallest droplet to the mightiest river, water works to shape landscape. River systems stitch together landscape, transporting materials and living organisms rather like our body's circulatory system. A catchment is a web of life. Healthy water bodies like wetlands and rivers are a highly complex web of natural system. Major engineering interventions such as dams, water diversions, and channelization and land reclamations across the rivers, lakes and wetlands projects harm drainage system by altering their chemistry, their flow, their physical nature (geomorphology). Natural river systems provide fisheries, floodplain agriculture, natural services and products, aquifer replacement, water quality improvement and high biodiversity—all free. All of these free services can be diminished or destroyed by wrong planning etc.

On the other hand, the global climate system is a consequence of and a link between the atmosphere, earth, ocean, ice, and the land. Any change in the link, resulting - climate change, is produced by forcing agents may be either internal or external. Global warming or cooling can be driven by an imbalance between the energy the Earth receives from the sun, largely as visible light, and the energy it radiates back to space as invisible infra-red. The greenhouse effect is caused by the presence in the air of gases and clouds that absorb some of the infra-red flowing upwards and radiate it back downwards. The large- scale problems of today's environmental change have been created by the abuse and overuse of the Earth's resources during the development of industrial society over the past three centuries. The over-exploitation of the water, air and land of the earth planet resulted in rise of sea level, species extinction, and loss of biodiversity, soil erosion and desertification.

The threats of climate change are widely aware by all nations today. The international community took serious initiatives to arrest the present day trend of global warming and climate change. The Convention on Climate Change, a United Nations framework, calls for stabilizing atmospheric concentrations of greenhouse gases at levels that will avoid critical destabilizations of global economies and ecosystems. Government and non-governmental organizations are currently engaged to make people aware of the threat and are taking actions to reduce the emissions of greenhouse gases.

The present book tries to focus some of the vital issues causing degradation of natural ecosystem in Manipur. Further it also highlights the better environmental planning and application of clean technology for a sustainable development. Here sustainable development means "*development which meets the needs of the present without compromising the ability of future generations to meet their own needs*". Some of the papers attempt to create awareness among the readers of the burning issues on the degradation of natural environment of Manipur including its causes, effects and control measures.

Authors

1

Manipur: A Land of Colourful Ethnic Mosaic

Geographically, Manipur is a unique land of Mountains with intermittent river valleys and plains. This area has been evolved with a typical natural environmental factor. Through this environmental framework, the area creates specific geo-climatic regions of endemic flora and fauna and an ideal home for the indigenous settlers. Identification with the shared experiences of like-minded groups, or cultures, within a familiar and stable territorial setting has, of course, been a natural process inherent in the history of human settlement in the present state of Manipur. Communities have come to inhabit at particular locational places and, over the centuries of occupation, have gradually come to identify with their regional or macro-environments, perceived as archetypal, endowed with love and celebrated in songs and poetry, as well as understood in terms of appropriate land use and economic development. The sense of national identity in its recognizable modern form took root and crystallized in a particular historical point of time in Manipur. Within these processes, minorities whose cultures were submerged or denied, preserved and nurtured their identities in whatever ways they could, towards the day when they would be able to flower freely again. In the meantime, self-determination, led to the birth, resurrection or amalgamation of many long-standing cultural groups into a new nation-state in Manipur. This may be equivalent with the young United States of America's experience of surge of new-found nationalism. However, the process of amalgamation of different ethnicities into one nation of Manipur was severely disturbed by the waves of Hindunization/Sanskritization or Indianization. Then, the process has been further aggravated by the colonization of the Britishers.

It seems reasonable to expect that the inevitable globalization of culture and economy after the Second World War and the rapid growth of communications would lead to a progressive dilution or even disappearance of national and regional identity feelings. It might also be expected that such an outcome would have been accelerated by the spread of 'multinational' capitalism and the accompanying tidal wave of English as a new international 'lingua franca'.

Even if the changing winds are blowing very fast all over the globe, there are certain areas like Manipur which could not be touched by the changing wave. Large or small ethnic groups of the state claim each other for a distinct socio-cultural identity and displaying ethnic psyche accompanied by such behavioral pattern as assertion of identity, seeking socio-cultural and economic protection, reservation, etc. All these have led to socio-political unrest in the state, especially during the last few decades. An analysis of the causes of ethnicity reveals the following points:

1. Different racial and ethno-linguistic origin, living earlier in different physical locational setting, came to life in the State of Manipur. Different groups of people, therefore, inherit different socio-cultural and racial identity.
2. Different groups of people, coming at different points of time, settled in different physiographic settings and hence, have been brought up by different socio-economic milieu. This process has given different identity to different groups.

3. Historical compulsions and developments were such that there was an ample opportunity for emotional integration of various people to form a single political hegemony of the state in the past. It is noteworthy to mention that the changes were nipped in the bud by the process of Indianization/Sanskritization. Further the British created Hills and Plains isolation imposing Hill administration-handling solely by them. This reinforced the isolation between the hills and the valley people.
4. During the British rule, as also merged with the Indian, there occurred unequal sectoral development. Development was more in some area and less or absent in some other areas. Then again, development was relatively quick in the field of general education but less in the economic sector. Furthermore, administrative exigency led to opening up of new area linking distant places. Such a situation has laid bare the painful fact of hill and valley economic disparities and social imbalances. The result is that the educated unemployed has been increasing with spatial differences and regional imbalances are realized grudgingly, with all their undesirable consequences.
5. Because of geographic isolation of certain hilly areas inhabited by certain ethnic groups and absence of development in them, there is a feeling of deprivation and exploitation among the people inhabiting in the State. On top of this, north-east India as a whole is physically almost isolated from the main-land India. As a result of these geographical facts, there exists a feeling of 'deprivation and exploitation' at different levels: Firstly, there is a feeling, among the people of the eastern Himalayas as a whole of being

'deprived and exploited by the centre. Secondly, the tribes feel that they are being deprived and exploited by the non-tribal people (or by the valley people to the highlanders). Thirdly, the backward and minority groups feel that they are being deprived and exploited by the relatively advanced majority groups. Fourthly, the same feeling is seen to prevail among the smaller tribes against the dominant tribes.

6. Unabated migration of people from even beyond the international boundary in the state has been continuing from such a long time and in such large volumes that the local people fear of being swamped and losing their cultural identity, political and economic hold. It is often found that the right and imaginative decisions and measures are not taken, letting an ethnic situation to be serious later on.

7. Lack of economic development in the state leading to rapid growth of unemployment, especially educated unemployment, has thrown the youths– both male and female – into a state of aimless atmosphere. Such a situation is taken advantage of by the people with vested political and selfish interests. These so-called leaders know that ethnicity is a powerful tool to unite a group of people. So they take advantage of it and arouse ethnic sentiments among the people of their respective ethnic groups at the cost of unity and integrity of the State of Manipur. The present day crisis of ethnic unrest is one of the most important problems hindering socio-economic growth and territorial integrity of the State. But the problems have to be solved. Firstly, the sense of deprivation and exploitation at all levels has to be wiped out through sincere efforts; Secondly,

the sense of insecurity and fear of indigenous small culture being swamped has to be contained, by making genuine efforts to contain immigration and allowing to grow all the individual indigenous ethnic culture of the State (Manipur Cultural Integration Conference's Approach); Thirdly, an action plan is to be taken up to empower the ethnic groups to develop their own culture, dialects and sustainable development of their specific locational factor; Fourthly, effort should be made to acquaint each ethnic groups which is established through understanding with the idea of peaceful co-existence; Fifthly, avenue should be created so that common people of both hills and plain be able to participate in all affairs of socio-economic and political development in the State.

These may require both long-term and short-term policies. But such policies can be found out if the ethnic leaders, politicians, welfare-bodies, socioeconomic planners and social engineers put heads together and make concerted efforts.

2

Everybody Lives Downstream

As viewed from space, Earth appears as a watery planet because nearly 71 per cent of its surface is covered by oceans/seas. All the water on Earth makes up what is called the hydrosphere. The origin of hydrosphere dated back to the beginning of Earth's history more than 4.5 billion years ago. At some early stage of the Earth's formation, it began to release water and various gases from its interior by a process known as degassing. Most of the water on Earth's surface is concentrated in the southern hemisphere where the water to land ratio is about 4 to 1 and the distribution of water differs from place to place and from region to region.

Nowadays, the problem of water is becoming increasingly acute mostly due to the unscientific exploration of available resources and also destruction of the natural environment. The problem is further aggravated due to the deterioration of quality of surface waters and their progressive pollution. However, a good deal of effort is being made to prevent this evil but its efficiency is so far inadequate. It is also realized that the basic cause of the environmental degradation and problem of water is mainly caused by the consequent effect of the continuous population growth and expansion of urbanization and its infrastructural activities at the cost of the Natural Physiographic regions.

The many proposals for rational use of water resources

and its conservation may be categorized into two basic groups. The first includes the study of universal principles of water cycle and global water budget while the second group deals with the assessment of the water resources and nature of utilization etc. For the rational use of the water resources and its conservation a fundamentally different approach is necessary for organizing the use of water resources and measures to protect them. The most important approach is the end of the abuse of water resources and proper taping of available resources for the whole mankind. To substantiate this concept, we shall try to prove first that the water resources available on earth, provided they are used prudently, can meet the requirements of mankind and, secondly, we shall outline the principal ways to safeguard and use them rationally.

The water resources consist of statistic resources of the hydrosphere and water continually reproduced in the process of their circulation. The water is found in the atmosphere on the earth's surface and within the crust of the earth. In the atmosphere, water is found in the warmest layer, the troposphere, either in vapours or solid state, or in the form of liquid droplets. Surface water, i.e. the water in oceans, seas, lakes, river, reservoirs and glaciers, is found either in liquid or solid state. Within the earth's crust i.e. within the lithosphere, water is found in vapours, liquid or solid state; moreover, it can be firmly or largely bound by rock particles, as well as bound chemically in crystal lattice of various minerals. Surface water, underground water and the water contained in the tissues of all animals and plants (Biosphere) together compose the water envelop of the earth usually called the Hydrosphere.

The total volume of resources of water at any given time is not great but, owing to water circulation, they assume tremendous importance for the life of human race. They refer primarily, to river water whose volume within river beds adds upto a mere 1,200 cu. km. However, owing to its extremely high mobility, river water renews in river beds once in 12 days on the average, or 30 times in one year. However, a major portion is polluted as a consequence of rapid industrialization and excessive population growth.

At one time no one questioned the amount of fresh and pure water present on this globe. After traveling for a long distance, a man did not have the slightest doubt in questioning his thirst with water from a nearby lake or river. The problem of the water being loaded with toxic chemicals or being heavily contaminated with the pathogenic microbes did not arise. Now, the whole scenario has changed completely. The problem of pollution is intensely acute in many parts of the world. Hundreds of rivers, lakes, streams and other water bodies in a country have now become polluted with all sorts of industrial, agricultural and domestic wastes, oil and city sewages laden with numerous pathogenic microbes. The world's industrial products now include more than 30,000 chemical substances and several hundred new substances of this type are added to the list each year. Public health authorities in many countries are greatly alarmed by various toxic chemical pollutants being discharged ultimately to various water bodies.

Access to a secure, safe and sufficient source of fresh water is a fundamental requirement for survival, well-being and socio-economic development of all humanity. It is high time to make aware that our human activities on the land are the major causes of both water shortages and water pollution. Agricultural development, urbanization, and industrialization cause the most harm and must be the primary focus of freshwater management efforts. Water is literally and figuratively fluid resources; actions within one part of the watershed can be a profound effect on human water use in other parts. We must learn that "everybody lives downstream".

Special attention may be given on the problem of

drinking water currently faced (March & April 1999) by the people of Manipur. During this spring season of 1999, on this part of the globe, people are struggling for a drop of potable water. On the contrary, Manipur geographically is located in a zone where the world's heaviest rainfall is recorded. At present, the State receives 142 cm of rain water annually. The total surface water resource of the State has been roughly estimated as 18,487 million hectare metres in the form of average annual yield. With this enough amount of water, people of Manipur both in the hills and valley are facing acute shortage of drinking water. Demand for drinking water is growing rapidly in the State and more particularly during the spring and pre-monsoon season. Simultaneously, increased water pollution is worsening the imbalance between water supply and demand. Hardly any river, pond or lake in the State today escapes pollution. As a result it is said that more than 75% of the common diseases occurring in the State are water borne diseases. Now water becomes every body's concern; a paradigm in which the household and the community will enter into a new relationship with an equal stake in water management.

The frequent occurrence of flood and drought alternately in the same year is the real index of the environmental condition or status of Environment in the State of Manipur. Whatever amount of rain received by the State was stored naturally by the forest in the distant past. Now almost all the forest coverage has been reduced disproportionately and hence all the rain water just turns into surface run-off with soil erosion, soil wash in the hill slopes and silation in the valley. Geographically, the State water resources and its water bodies were under one biome i.e. the hills of Manipur is the source of water and watershed area of the State. It is really unfortunate that the State has singular habit of not making use of its available water resources. By 2001 A.D. Manipur will be able to use only a tenth of the total annual rain, and hence it is speculated that we would face the threat of water shortages in the decades to come. The reason for this is simply that we cannot hold on to all the water the State receives. More than 80% of the monsoon water disappears through surface run-off and evaporation etc. Now let us prepare for a rational use of water and conservation of water in the light of the United Nations theme of World Water Day i.e., "Everybody Lives Downstream" and the "World Water Vision Project".

3

Forest and Environment

Introduction

Forests are vitally important in economic, social, ecological and cultural terms, both locally and nationally and for the development of the State. In the State, forests help to meet the basic needs of the local population and indigenous people in particular, and are the basis for their economic and social development. Forests are home to most of the endemic biological diversity together with the wetlands where they regulate the hydrological and carbon cycles and hence regulate the climatic condition of the State. It is of paramount importance that this far reaching function be preserved, and the contribution of forests to sustainable development guaranteed.

Forest and environment of Manipur, in the recent past, was one of the most luxuriant and resourceful in the country. This has been reflected in all the cultural ethos and way of lives of every Manipuri in the State. The forest and its environmental factors of this State have continuously cherished culturally refined quality of human development in terms of art and culture, sports and martial activities and varieties of folk literature. Knowing the role of forest and environment, the then native rulers preserved and protected the natural heritages of the State with their traditional humble practices. It is also presumed that the most refined cultural epitomes were projected during those days of luxuriant forest vis-à-vis environment condition of the State. During the last seven decades the forest and environmental conditions have been adversely degraded. It may, however, be described that population growth and distribution patterns of the State have significant roles to play in the sustainability of the available natural resources. Not only the increasing number of people, but also the changing life style and consumption patterns directly affect the forest environment condition of the State. Thus, consequently affecting the ongoing development of human resources of the State.

> "What now remains of the rich land is like the skeleton of a sick man, all the fat and soft each has wasted away, only the bare framework is left. Formerly, many of the present mountains were arable hills, the present mashes were plain fill of rich soils; hills were covered with forest, and produced boundless pasturage that now produce only food for bees. Moreover, the land was enriched by yearly rains which were not lost, as now by flowing from the bare land into the sea the soil was deep ill received water, storing in the retentive loamy soil . . . ." (Critias, quoted from Bridges and Davidson 1982).

Its coordinating location, its topographic landscaping and corresponding climate and soil condition of the area mainly determine the type of forest and its classification. The State is located in a tri-junction zone of mainland Indian sub-continent, Himalayan and Trans-Himalayan and Indo-Malayan genesis. A wide range of natural heritages of rare and endemic species of flora and fauna are visible in the State. The richness in natural heritage is the product of its geographical location and peculiar topographic exposition of drainage pattern and wetland systems of the State.

Topographically the State may be grouped into two physiographic units, namely the valley of Manipur and the surrounding mountain ranges. The valley of Manipur comprises the entire plain region of the Imphal East, Imphal West, Bishnupur, Thoubal and river valleys extensions of the Sadar Hills sub-division of Senapati and part of Churachandpur and Chandel Districts. The valley is approximately 2640 sq.km and dotted with a number of wetland and glittering lakes including the biggest fresh water take of the eastern India i.e. the Loktak Lake (Ramsar Site). The valley represents hardly 20 p.c. of the State's total geographical area of 22,327 sq.km. The 1000 meters contour is taken as the outer limit of the valley of Manipur. More than 75% of the total human population of the State is concentrated in the valley.

The hilly or mountainous region occupies a large portion of the state with an area of 19,687 sq.km. which is about 80% of the State's total geographical area with elevation ranging from 1000 m.a.m. S.L. to 3000 m.a.m. S.L. The Mt. Essii is the highest peak (3002 m) while Dzuku Valley the highest dale (2500 m) of the State.

The State is located in the entire catchment area of two major river systems namely the Ganga-Brahmaputra and the Chindwin-Irrawaddi. The western half of the State falls in the catchment areas of the Barak drainage system of the former river system while the remaining eastern half including the valley of Manipur lies in the catchment area of the Manipur River system of the Chindwin-Irrawaddi drainage system there are a number of wetlands. In all the interflures region of the Manipur River system of the Valley region. The existence of number of wetlands in the Manipur valley itself influences the microclimatic condition of the State.

Climatically, the state occupies the world's heaviest rainfall region and belongs to the monsoonal track of the world. During the recent past, the climate of Manipur was one of the most pleasant and celeberic conditions throughout the year. There are two seasons separated by two transitions.

Further, the climate of Manipur may be classified into the following regions: -

1. Sub-tropical monsoonal rainforest climate: which is wet and hot summer with dry winter. It covers the valley areas as well as low-lying foothill regions, where sub-tropical and tropical semi-evergreen forests predominantly occur.
2. Sub-tropical monsoonal highland temperate climate: which, is characterized by wet mild summer and dry cold winter. It covers all the highland regions of mountainous hilly tracts where tropical moist deciduous forests with secondary growth and sub-topical fine forests occur.

Based on the topographic and micro-climatic conditions, the forests of Manipur have been classified as in Table 1.

TABLE 1

Forest Type

Sl. No.	*Type of Forest*	*Area in Sq. km.*
(i)	Wet Temperate Forest (11 BC)	1451.01
(ii)	Sub-tropical Pine Forest ($9C_2$)	2442.77
(iii)	Sub-tropical Wet Hill Forests ($23/C_2$)	6590.59
(iv)	Tropical Semi-evergreen Forests ($23/C_2$)	644.89
(v)	Teak Gurjan Forests ($2B/C_2$)	610.74
(vi)	Bamboo Brakes	3268.00
(vii)	Grass Brakes	146.00

The aerial photo imaging conducted by the pre-investment survey (1976) of forest resources, government of India has shown the classification of land use as in Table 2.

TABLE 2

Land Use 1976

Sl. No.	Category	Area in Sq. km.
(i)	Forest	15,154.94
(ii)	Agri-tree Land	337.10
(iii)	Crop Land	3,170.72
(iv)	Current Jhum	1,832.08
(v)	Urban Sites	193.13
(vi)	Pasture & Barren Land	1,578.03

N.B.: 61 sq.km. not reported.

Subsequently, as per Land use project Manipur State Remote Sensing Centre. Directorate of Science, Technology and Environment, Government of Manipur (1990) published the following land use classification and land cover categories:

TABLE 3

Land Use 1990

Sl. No.	Category	Area (in hect.)	% to State Total Area
I.	Settlement	54,520.00	2.44
II.	Agriculture Land	1,48,527.62	6.65
III.	Forest Cover	10,99,590.30	49.25
IV.	Land with or without Scrub	8,64,612.80	38.72
V.	Water Bodies	36,824.63	1.65
VI.	Others	28,579.75	1.29
	Total	22,32,655.10	100.00

TABLE 4

Vegetation

Sl. No.	Vegetation Type	Area in Sq. Km.
I.	Coniferous Forest	2,442.00
II.	Non-Coniferous (Broad Leaved)	9,444.00
III.	Pure Bamboo Brakes	3,268.00
	Total	15,154.00

Source: Forest Dept. Manipur Govt., 1986.

According to Forest Survey of India (Report 1997) the total forest area of the State is 17,418 sq. km. of which the recorded forest area is approximately 15,154 sq. km. During 1995 to 1997 the area under dense forest has been reduced form 5318 sq. km. to 4937 sq. km. while the open forest area increases from 12240 sq. km. to 12481 sq. km. The net loss was 140 sq. km. i.e. at the rate of 20 hectares per day approximately. (20 m^2 of timber per day on average) 'I' here are certain cases where the figure of forest area estimated by the revenue Department, State Remote Sensing Department and the Department of Forest found conflicting each other. The difference in the estimation calls for a greater coordination between the government agencies. The Environment and Ecology Wing of the Department of Forest should initiate to strengthen the coordination between these institutions like Forest, Agriculture and Revenue working on forest related environmental issues in Manipur. It is also a fact that forests are central to livelihood of the people of Manipur, is confirmed by the existence of many traditional and customary forest laws etc.

Socio-culturally, based on the customary land laws, most of the land area inhabited by the indigenous hilly people has been grouped into four distinct classifications as stated below:-

1. Settlement area (Homestead land centrally located).
2. Individual household plot (Tree & vegetable cropping area surrounding the settlement area).
3. Cranial land (Preserving good varieties of wood and trees surrounding the second classification).
4. Village/community/public land (Jhumming area surrounding the 3rd classification of land).

The first classified land i.e. settlement area is used only for construction of dwelling houses and domestic animal shed. The second classified land is distributed to each and every individual household for any kind of activities, which is related to his livelihood. The third classified land belongs to the head of the clan. However, individual member of the clan may utilize the plot with due permission from the clanial head. The outermost surrounding land i.e. the

TABLE 5

Legal Classification of Forests

Sl. No.	*Classification*	*Area in sq. km.*	*P.C.*
I.	Reserved Forest	1,467	8.4
II.	Protected Forest	4,171	24.0
III.	Unclassified Forest	11,780	76.6

Source: Forest Department, Government of Manipur.

TABLE 6

Office/Divisionwise Major and Minor Forest 1998-1999

Office/Divn.	*Major Forest Produce Revenue*	*Minor Forest Produce Revenue*	*Misc. Revenue*	*Total*
CCF/General	Nil	Nil	58,345.00	58,345.00
CCF/Wildlife	Nil	Nil	1,401.00	1,401.00
CF/HQ	Nil	13,69,166.00	41,341.00	14,10,507.00
DFO/Jiribam	300.00	2,51,545.00	1,50,350.00	4,02,195.00
DFO/Rubber	Nil	5,51,800.00	Nil	5,51,800.00
DFO/West	1,920.00	90,349.00	Nil	92,269.00
DFO/South	1,35,390.00	69,368.00	Nil	2,04,758.00
DFO/East	2,79,278.00	17,060.00	48,996.00	3,45,334.00
DFO/North	90,958.00	3,63,528.00	Nil	4,54,334.00
DFO/Chandel	19,26,234.00	47,544.00	4,280.00	19,78,058.00
DFO/Thoubal	920.00	43,407.00	Nil	44,327.00
DFO/Bishnupur	11,171,55.00	63,133.00	Nil	74,304.55
DFO/Central	50,590.00	12,41,210.00	2,000.00	12,93,800.00
DFO/Zoo	Nil	Nil	1,35,641.00	1,35,641.00
	Total =	**70,47,225.55**		

fourth classified land area belongs to the village where individual household may practice Jhum and other economic activities. Thus, there are definite hill people's sociological factors controlling the use of available land and forest of their respective villages. Forest covers much of the geographical area of the State. They are extremely important to human and natural world of the people of Manipur. Forests of Manipur have aesthetic recreational economic, historical, cultural and religious value. Even today forests are an important source of livelihood for the Manipuri people. Apart from the extraction of timber and fuel woods, forest is also the source of varieties of plants, herbs, and orchids that have been traditionally used as medicines, food and cultural items of the people of Manipur. As well as, for example, Timber and other products of forest are important economically both locally and as exports.

TABLE 7

Office/Divisionwise Major and Monor Forest (1999-2000)

Office/Divn.	*Major Forest Produce Revenue*	*Minor Forest Produce Revenue*	*Misc. Revenue*	*Total*
CCF/General	Nil	Nil	16,820.00	16,820.00
CCF/Wildlife	Nil	Nil	1,355.00	1,355.00
CF/HQ	Nil	31,63,994.00	14,558.00	31,78,552.00
DFO/Jiribam	2,275.00	6,57,533.00	3,79,225.00	10,39,033.00
DFO/Rubber	Nil	9,93,200.00	Nil	9,93,200.00
DFO/West	Nil	2,00,082.00	Nil	2,00,082.00
DFO/South	4,20,211.00	1,23,834.00	3,914.00	5,74,959.00
DFO/East	5,46,438.00	9,800.00	Nil	5,56,238.00
DFO/North	7,24,541.00	2,39,364.00	Nil	9,63,977.00
DFO/Chandel	4,85,883.00	1,39,436.00	8,453.00	6,33,600.00
DFO/Thoubal	10,080.00	65,350.00	Nil	75,430.00
DFO/Bishnupur	11,250.00	12,000.00	Nil	23,250.00
DFO/Central	1,17,618.00	9,47,875.00	1,71,910.00	12,37,403.00
DFO/Zoo	Nil	Nil	2,06,834.00	2,06,834.00
	Total =	**97,00,733.00**		

TABLE 8

Office/Divisionwise Major And Minor Forest (2000-2001)

Office/Divn.	*Major Forest Produce Revenue*	*Minor Forest Produce Revenue*	*Misc. Revenue*	*Total*
CCF/General	Nil	Nil	76,754.00	76,754.00
CCF/Wildlife	Nil	Nil	50.00	50.00
CF/HQ	Nil	6,14,904.00	1,68,576.00	7,83,480.00
DFO/Jiribam	2,280.00	14,31,952.00	1,880.00	14,35,112.00
DFO/Rubber	Nil	Nil	Nil	Nil
DFO/West	570.00	2,23,738.00	Nil	2,24,318.00
DFO/South	3,95,514.00	76,900.00	200.00	4,72,614.00
DFO/East	1,41,163.00	34,600.00	1,77,005.00	3,52,768.00
DFO/North	4,37,160.00	2,11,802.00	Nil	6,48,962.00
DFO/Chandel	16,99,372.00	96,478.00	21,950.00	18,17,800.00
DFO/Thoubal	44,490.00	1,17,065.00	Nil	1,61,555.00
DFO/Bishnupur	13,040.55	20,655.00	Nil	33,695.00
DFO/Central	2,05,527.00	9,69,322.00	5,700.00	11,80,549.00
DFO/Zoo	Nil	Nil	1,56,679.00	1,56,679.00
	Total =	**73,44,326.00**		

TABLE 9

Office/Divisionwise Major and Minor Forest (2001-2002)

Office/Divn.	*Major Forest Produce Revenue*	*Minor Forest Produce Revenue*	*Misc. Revenue*	*Total*
CCF/T & P	Nil	Nil	4,71,500.00	4,71,500.00
CF/Adm&Plg.	Nil	1,86,028.00	13,20,248.00	15,06,276.00
DFO/Jiribam	20..00	8,19,086.00	3,325.00	8,22,431.00
DFO/West	Nil	1,48,322.00	Nil	1,48,322.00
DFO/South	7,90,004.00	1,04,155.00	Nil	8,94,159.00
DFO/East	5,45,080.00	20,610.00	12,409.00	5,78,099.00
DFO/North	2,62,869.00	2,98,078.00	Nil	5,60,947.00
DFO/Chandel	4,05,478.00	62,731.00	24,620.00	4,92,829.00
DFO/Thoubal	68,340.00	2,42,085.00	Nil	3,10,425.00
DFO/Bishnupur	40,080.55	37,145.00	Nil	77,225.00
DFO/Central	2,68,891.00	14,14,188.00	18,700.00	17,01,779.00
DFO/Zoo	Nil	Nil	18,8,634.00	1,88,634.00
	Total =	**97,00,733.00**		

They provide employment to those who harvest the wood or products of living forest. Herbalists, hunters and collectors of fungi, nuts and bamboo are able to utilize such resources. Other non-wood forest products come in the form of medicinia compounds, dyes and fabrics. Majority of the people of Manipur depend on wood for fuel as a significant energy source. Recent studies show that increasing consumption of higher levels of education and other indicators of social development. However, energy consumption of fuel wood as a source of energy is commonly contrary to the above findings. This higher energy consumption may also fail to produce economic growth if there are no examples of substantial economic growth without corresponding growth in energy consumption, but of changing the kinds of energy used. The energy consumption of the poor is inefficient, polluting and unhealthy. Per unit of emitted light or heat, the poor pay higher price than the rich, including the time they spent in obtaining or collecting fuel. Gathering fuel-wood and related materials takes its toll in time and injury, mostly on women. Failure to cook food or boil water adequately because of fuel shortage or inefficiency also contributes to malnutrition, intestinal disorders and parasites. Almost all the highland indigenous people are completely dependent on forest wildlife for animal protein source and other livelihood. Over and above this the availability of resources of the forest influences the art and craft skill development of the Human resources of the State. *Forest is one of the potential growth areas of Manipur, where cultivation of medicinal plants like Panax pseudo-ginseng, coptis teeta wall, Taxus baccata Linn, Kaemferia rotunda L., Goniotilulamus sesquipedalis lhook. F., etc.* and also extraction of steroidal drugs from the varieties of bamboos of the State could be an important source of revenue to the Government. Similarly, crisis of the cooking energy shortage may be recouped based on the cheap availability of bamboos of the State. At the same time attention should be given to protecting the intellectual property rights of the communities, whose indigenous world market. Subsequently, the role of forest for overall maintenance of local climate environment of the State, invites more attention.

BOX-1

Biological Diversity

4000 angiospermic plants
500 orchids
55 bamboo species
40 endemic rice cultivars
160 fish species
21 wild birds
20 medicinal zingberales
Multitudes of low/high altitude
Butterflies – bee diversities etc.

Scientific Floristic studies of the State of Manipur were recorded since 1889. Watt reported 143 plant species, Clarke reported 1050 flowering plants and 114 ferns of which 422 species are from Manipur, Deb (1957, 1961) reported 1500 plant species, Baishya and Sukla (1984) reported 43 new species of flowering plants and 13 cryptogerms from Manipur, A.C. Sinha (1987) added 523 plant species, Bikram added 667 plant species, Kumar (2001) reported 31 wild edible plant species. Based on this information and with the application of Science and Technology like Gamplasm/ Tissue Culture technique the field scientists may extend the laboratory information to the field culture so that new stream of revenue generation may be projected for the State in this context, a tripartite coordination among the Educational/Research Institutions, the Government Departments and the NGOs or voluntary organizations. As for example, the State may initiate commercialization of orchid or Medicinal plants etc. by negotiating Manipur University's Life Sciences Department or Central Agricultural University to establish laboratory for Tissue culture/

Ganiplasm to produce plantlets with the legal and resource support by the Department of Forest. After that the plantlets be allowed to culture by expertised/trained NGOs in the field of forest and the product can be commercially exported for earning income.

Forest Revenue

Forest is one of the most important sources of revenue for the state of Manipur. However, there are a number of scopes for percolating the revenue before reaching the State Revenue account. It may be because of dereliction of duty by concerned authority and avoidance of performing the responsibilities of the concerned citizens etc. Therefore, the total expenditure for conservation and development of forests is far in excess of the total revenue received from the forest products and in terms of attributing to the conservation of natural environment of the State. The highest share in the revenues earned from forest both minor and major products, was Rs. 29,653.00 in the year 1997-98. But it has been declining in the subsequent years (*Statistical Handbook of Manipur*, 2002). On the other hand the quantity of forest product has also been continuously going down. During 1965-66 the timber quantity was 18,000 cubic meters and has been reduced to 2,000 cubic meters in the year 2000-01. Similarly the production of fuel wood has also been reduced from 210,000 cubic meters in the year 1975-76 to 27000 cubic meters in the year 2000-01.

It may be very difficult to quantify the amount in terms of value contributed by the forest to the people of Manipur including all the livestock populations, etc. However, every one is concerned to preserve and protect the forest for our betterment and legacy to our generations to come.

The relationship between population growth and environmental degradation in the State appears to be rather straightforward. A gradual shift from very low to moderate population densities, for example, can encourage new agricultural practices, providing increased yields and supporting larger populations. Such a process may have encouraged the development of intensive settled agriculture. Increasing rural population density increases the labour force and also infrastructural facilities such as irrigation canals and terraces, and improving soils. On the other hand, more people demand more resources and generate more waste. Clearly, one of the challenges of a growing population is the continuous increase of population growth and sharing extremely limited resources available in the State straining its natural environment.

Continuing improvements in agricultural yields and quality of life depend on the complex interplay of environmental conditions, availability of appropriate technology and social organization and on choices concerning land use. Higher densities require successive adaptations to new circumstances. Eventually, further progress may be constrained by natural limits, for example on water for irrigation; by technological consequences such as soil degradation from repeated use of chemical fertilizers, by political decisions concerning land use and social organization, or by economic factors such as poverty.

Intensive agriculture has increased yield in many rural areas of the State, but it has provided cheap food for increasing urban populations, rather than a living for rural populations. Commercial agriculture and timber and fuel wood operations by individuals on common land can be highly profitable as long as inputs are available and resources last, but the benefits rarely go to local communities. The rural and hilly poor are often using, and overlying whatever land, water and forest resources are left over from commercial exploitations. The combined results can be seen in bare hill slopes and catchments areas of the State, shrinking watercourse and wetlands in the valley, floods, droughts and vanishing wildlife.

Further we are also well aware that the state is located in the region where the world's heaviest rainfall is recorded. On the contrary, the state is facing insufficient safe drinking water for its inhabitants. Most of the peasants are suffering from lack of sufficient agricultural water and also of excess water. Every year the state is facing problems of flood and droughts alternately during the same year. As a result the agrarian economy particularly in the rural sections is seriously hampered. On the other hand, the biggest fresh water Loktak Lake has been continuously degraded both by the development activities and also by the growth of population and urbanization. After the implementation and commission of Loktak Hydro Electric Project, the natural environment condition of the lake has totally degraded. As a result, the occupational and cultural heritages generated by the Loktak Lake have also been adversely altered. Almost all the paddy fields were becoming useless except to change the paddy cultivation to fishery. Even for the fishes these peasants shall have to take fishing pond or bunds encircling their respective areas but were not been able to invest properly. It is also worthwhile to mention herewith that after the commission of the Ithai Barrage, the water level of the Loktak has raised permanently at a certain level. Traditionally and naturally Loktak water rises during monsoon and low down during the lean season. During these raise and fall of the Loktak water level the fishing community of the lake was allowed two fishing seasons by using their traditional techniques. Since the lake water is stagnant and kept at a certain level now, the traditional fishing technique could not be deployed by the fishing community. And hence, some of the fishing population used fault practice including application of carcinogenic pesticide into the lake water. Therefore it is high time to alert all the state machineries and planners to provide appropriate technology to these communities for both developments of human resources in and around the wetland complex of the state.

Recent studies of Green Revolution in our country reveal that increased productivity has led to greater incentive to expand area under cultivation. Where forests and virgin lands are owned in common, this has led to deforestation in the hill slopes and reclamation of wetlands in the valley, because there is no control over the use of common land. Other studies have shown that the benefits of the Green Revolution have occurred principally to the affordable groups/individuals and users of common resources, presumably because they had the most to invest and the most to gain. Landless among former subsistence farmers and impoverishment by loss of common resources have been unlooked – for consequences of the green revolution.

BOX 2

Decadal Population in Manipur

Census Year	*Population*	*Geographical Area In Sq. Km.*	*Density Sq. Km.*	*No. of Towns*
1901	2,84,463	22,437	13	1
1911	3,46,222	22,437	15	1
1921	3,48,016	22,437	17	1
1931	4,45,606	22,437	20	1
1941	5,77,635	22,437	23	1
1951	5,77,635	22,437	26	1
1961	7,80,037	22,346	35	1
1971	10,72,753	22,356	48	8
1981	14,20,953	22,327	64	32
1991	18,37,149	22,327	82	31
2001	23,88,634	22,327	107	33

Source: Statistical Handbook of Manipur – 2002.

While looking at the impact of human activities, the situation is more complicated due to the wide variety of government policies, technologies, and worldwide consumption patterns. High level of consumption, inequality in wealth, land distribution, inappropriate government policies on land use, poverty, inefficient technologies and lack of public distribution system in Manipur contribute to the process of environmental degradation. In this context, deforestation had been the most critical environmental danger for the delicate fragile eco-system of Manipur. Even then, rural and highlanders will continue to depend heavily on agriculture and natural resources for their livelihood. Environmental degradation will only deepen their poverty, so environmental conservation and poverty alleviation programme are parallel objective. In most situations where they enjoy secure tenure, the poor will invest to protect their land and their environment.

On the other hand, over the generations rural and hill dwellers have accumulated a vast amount of knowledge about sustainable environmental practices. Practices such as shifting cultivation sustained the poor for centuries, until population grew too large or other factors intervened. Traditional practices may incorporate an understanding of local conditions not immediately evident to outside observers, however expert. In the hilly region of Manipur, Jhummias followed their age old traditional practices based on their customary land laws for a quite long time. However, currently the customary land laws are becoming extremely stretches and strain so that preservation of moth trees in the Jhum field, wildfire protection of forest belt of the core settlement area are all degraded. As a result the State's forest conditions have fallen under critical concern areas and as such immediate conservational measures are necessary.

BOX–3

Shifting Cultivation/Jhumming/Pamlou

Shifting cultivation popularly known as Jhumming or Pamlou in Manipur is considered the first step in transition from food-gathering or hunting to food production. This system of land-use is believed to have originated in the Neolithic period around 7000 B.C. This type of age-old land-use system is still in vogue in the hill districts of Manipur. Jhumming cultivations is tightly associated with the activities of slash and burn technique by cutting forest, cleaning of green vegetation of the selected hill slope, areas, drying and burning the same prior to thriving of crops' seeds.

No drought power or improved technology is deployed by the Jhummias for the cultivation. The only implement used in the farming are the chopping knife, dibbling stick and small hoe for weeding. The only inputs used are seeds and human labour. Except cutting of forests and watching to protect the crops, the other labour operation including weeding are usually carried out by women. All essential crops, such as paddy, maize, tapioca, colocsia, sesame, curarbits beans, yams, pumkin and plantain etc. are planted in an intimate mixture, although a monocrop of paddy is sometimes grown in the second year of Jhumming. The Jhum land is left fallow for rejuvenation of green coverage after 2 to 3 years of Jhum used. Under this process more than 900 sq. km. of forested area has been transformed into Jhum-field annually. Further by the increase of population growth and expansion of infrastructural facilities of urbanization the Jhum cycle has been shortened from 20-30 years to 2-3 years by now.

One of the most serious challenges in the State today comes from the deforestation in the strategic catchment areas of the two major river systems of the State. The challenge can be better understood if one recognizes the rate of deforestation, expansion of Jhum field, reduction of Jhum cycle with consequent effect to the down streams. Forest loss index, presence of 'hot spots' and biodiversity in the state are serious concerns of the day; Manipur losts more than 900 sq. km. of forest annually. Subsequently the Jhum cycle has also been reduced from 30 years in 1950's to 7 years in 1970 and finally 3 years to most of the Jhumming places currently.

The slash-and-burn agriculture and logging are continuously expanding in all the hilly regions of the State. Under unrelenting population pressure, subsistence farmers have stripped forest cover from the hill terrain of the State. The poor are the most visible agents of destruction in degraded environments. Poor people depend heavily on natural resources for direct income and their poverty offers them few choices. There is no appropriate alternative that the poor people could switch on for their immediate income generation. Here and elsewhere, the poor stands at the end of a long chain of cause and effect. They are the messengers of understandability rather than its gain. Therefore, it is high time to modernize the Jhumming practices to adjust it along with the present day environmental problems.

The depletion of forest resources has a wide-ranging impact on ecological balance ranging from the extinction of rare and endemic flora and fauna, siltation and drying of lakes and wetlands in the valley to local climate changes. Deforestation can cause the climate to become more extreme in nature. The occurrence of frequent floods followed by drought conditions in the same year has been experiencing by the people of Manipur during the last few decades.

On the other hand, the State is geographically located in a zone where the world's heaviest rainfall is recorded. At present, the State receives 142 cm. rainfall annually. It receives rain during the summer monsoon, from the middle of June through to September. During these four months it receives 60 p.c. of the total annual rainfall. However, because of the various environmental problems, the people of the State faces the problem of water i.e. droughts in lean seasons and flood in the peak seasons. Increase in the rate of deforestation accelerates surface runoff, soil wash/erosion and siltation in riverbed and lakes in the valley.

It is worth mentioning here that there were about 500 lakes and wetlands in Manipur Valley. Now, most of them become shallow or have dried up and are encroached upon by the ever-increasing human population. Special mention needs to be made here of the Loktak Lake, the biggest fresh water lake in the northeast India. Since the last couple of decades it has been consistently shrinking. 30 p.c. of the natural water area of the Loktak Lake has already shrunk. Despite huge investments of money in Loktak Multipurpose Project, the average projected land to be brought under irrigation is marginal and power generation has not proved to be profitable in the context of year long load-shedding in the State. High siltation as well as pollution of Loktak water poses a threat to the people and environment of the State and in the peripheral villages in particular.

The negative impact of the degradation of Loktak Lake is clearly discernible from the predicament of the fishing community. For the normal functioning of Loktak Hydro Electric Project, the water level of the lake has to be maintained at a particular level throughout the year. Resultantly, it has caused serious difficulty and misery for fishing community who concentrate in the peripheral villages of the lake. At one stroke, they have been deprived of their traditional techniques of fishing. There is also enough evidence of misuse of heavy doses of insecticides and pesticides being committed in the fresh water for the purpose of catching fishes. The fish thus caught are marketed in Manipur, causing health hazards and occasional deaths. This is one such evidence that the devastating consequences for the men and nature of the State notice today. This indicates the irresponsibility of the developmental plan like Loktak Hydro Electric Project etc. The ill-conceived implementation of projects has resulted in all round destruction rather than development. As a result these human potential growths in general in the State were made disorder.

Today, the people directly affected by the Loktak Project have become volatile about the grave danger to their existence. Under such circumstances to develop human resources of the State needs detailed examination.

Additionally, in the villages on hills and foothills, women and children spend a large part of their time traveling long distances to collect firewood and water. In some of the hill areas, the women folk walk up and down at least 10 kms, three out of four days, for an average of 7 hours per day to fetch 25 kg of wood in each headload. Children of the area become the unwitting victims of the continuous energy and water hunger in the villages on the hill and rural areas. Most of their prime time/man days are exhausted in the tasks of water and fuel gathering. In small towns, poor families spend a much larger proportion of their income on gathering their energy needs, often as much as 15 to 25 p.c. of their income. Besides, these poor families need to spend 80 to 90 per cent of their income on food and rising fuel cost automatically leads to reduced food intake. For an already malnourished population, this indeed is not simply unfortunate but a threat to their right to life. Most of these problems outlined above are virtually directly related to the degradation of forest and environment in our small State. To pull up Manipur in the ladder of economic growth or to say human development, Manipur should arrest its fast degrading environment and eco-system both in the hills, valleys and wetlands so that its economy does not sag or even collapse by 2020 A.D. by the sear weight of her fast growing population which is in a slightly better position than of the over all national average.

BOX - 4

Indigenous Knowledge System

I. Traditional Land Use on the Hill Slope of Khamkhui Village of Ukhrul District.

II. Terraces of Mao people.

III. Sacred Groves of Valley.

IV. Conservation of Bio-resources.

Through a long history of human settlement both in the hills and plain of Manipur the indigenous people evolved a typical kind of systems which shows a close relationship with the NATURE. The close relationship with nature, both in terms and struggle against the vagaries of nature and peaceful co-existence with nature, that has led, through a very long period of evolution of the indigenous culture and civilization. It is a matter of pride for us that till recently this moral order, a mutually respecting and mutually sustaining relationship with nature existed, among our indigenous people in this tiny state of Manipur. Some of the selected success stories of our indigenous people's knowledge systems are mentioned herewith for learning by the present generation with scientific interpretation.

I Khamkhui System of Land Use in the Hill Slope:

Khamkhui, a Tangkhul village of Ukhrul District is located in a limestone belt. This village is famous for Khamkhui Cave a lime stone cavern with stalactite and stalagmite features. This village has a traditional and age-old land use code evolved by the people of the area. The villagers always protect the top of the hills and mountains as a forest canopy area while the middle of the hill-slopes are used as settlement area with all domestic activities and lowermost foot-hill slopes are used for cultivation. This tradition is still in practice since time immemorial and since the evolution settlement of the Khamkhui Tangkhul. This type of land classification has a scientific implication. If the top of the hills and mountains are preserved as forested zone, the area will be the best and ideal water shed area and hence during the monsoon, rain water will be allowed to percolate down to the layers of the soil and thereby enriching the under water resources of the area and also maintaining the optimum water table of the area. This will influence the perennial source of water for domestic consumption as well as maintaining the soil moisture and maintaining a moderate climate in the area.

So long as the tops of the hills are protected with forest the community will settle with durably in the middle slope of the hill ranges. In the settlement area horticulture, kitchen gardening, poultry, piggery are successfully practiced. The byproduct of domestic waste, poultry and animal husbandry wastes are transformed into soil nutrient automatically to the foot-hill slopes where paddy cultivation is practiced. This is one of the most remarkable knowledge systems of the indigenous people of the Khamkhui Tangkhul to be learnt by the scientific communities. However, in the late 70's the ICAR developed a model of three tire system of land-use in the hills as follows:-

The topmost portion of the hill will be preserved/conserved for forestry and watershed management. The middle portion of the hill shall be for settlement cum horticulture cum animal cum buddy activities.

The lowermost portion or foot-hill areas are only meant for agricultural practice.

This model symbol perhaps is almost same as traditionally used by the indigenous highlanders of Khamkhui of Ukhrul District.

BOX – 5

(2) Traditional Land Use System of Purul Akutpa (Senapati District)

Purul Akutpa is a traditional village of Paomai tribe of Manipur settling in the upper catchments area of the Barak River. The indigenous people of Purul Akutpa practice, a typical land use system since time immemorial that they practice agri-cum-pisciculture in their paddy fields. The transplantation of paddy has been associated with one of the biggest annual festivals of "Paokee". On the night of Paokee, unmarried youths perform friendly fights with traditional wrestling art. On that particular night hour of friendly match of wrestling, it is the desire of the unmarried females to observe silently for selecting their probable life partner. Next morning after Paokee night all the women folk will work in the paddy field for transplantation. During the course of paddy transplantation unmarried males will join the female transplanters and negotiate for their life partnership. Hence the traditional land-use and cropping practices in the lower slope of the Purul Akutpa has been practicing with their matrimonial life. This helps the village a sustainable way of life.

Secondly, the Paomai of Purul Akutpa traditionally believed that if a family could erect big boulders in the form of monolithic culture in their paddy field then the production of the field is increased. It is also believed that if there are enough of big boulders the area is able to provide adequate water to the community. This may also be correlated with maintaining of optimum soil humidity for boosting the paddy productions in the area as believed by the indigenous people of the area.

BOX - 6

Terrace Field of Mao - Songsong

Through learning by experience, people of "Mao-Songsong, Pudunamei and Punanamei realize the significance of Terrace type of paddy field. They commonly cultivate paddy in the terrace field while the slopes are used for other crops and vegetables. While preparing the hill slope land for cultivation they always preserve the parent trees. If the oldest parent trees are able to be preserved in the Jhumfield, the productivity of that particular land has been increased. However, the oldest parent trees are nitrogen fixing trees commonly grown in the area. The system of terracing is as old as the evolution settlement in Songsong, Pudunamei and Punanamei. Hence, the indigenous knowledge system of the area is extremely significant for the sustainable human development of the area.

BOX - 7

Indigenous Conservation Practices

Indigenous people of the State of Manipur, living in some of the most remote and inaccessible villages are engaged in observing our natural heritage and its diversity even today. For example, in some of our villages, the people were found to be using at least fifteen (15) different varieties of local hill rice cultivars for thriving in the Jhumfields. These varieties of paddy were most sustainable for the prevailing local conditions, economic activities and consumption patterns. These traditional, age-old methods of cultivation and seed preservation are much more superior and sophisticated than the modern techniques and inputs. The total seeds and plants are free from diseases. This is one of the most successful stories of local people and their heritage. Apart from the rice cultivars recorded, a large variety of medicinal herbs and plants are still preserved by the local people for their home remedies and life aids.

Similarly, almost all the lowland dwellers in the valley maintain and protect some areas as sacred groves for the village a or clan's ancestral deity. This tradition has been practiced continuously since the evolution of valley settlement. Each clan or village has its own sacred groves sites and totem animals and plants are considered to be holy and hence, protected religiously.

In their sacred groves or protected forests, no one is permitted to touch the plant or tree or being living in them. This restriction is enforced as a social taboo as well, so the protective mechanisms are quite elaborate and complex. As a result, in the recent past, almost all the forests of the 'Umang Lai' were found to be the ideal zones for the protection and conservation of our priceless biologically diverse hedge. Simultaneously, a number of occupational and cultural activities, or in short all kinds of cultural waves and patterns, are generated as living heritage of the indigenous lowland dwellers of Manipur. All these cultural patterns and ethos clearly reflect an adaptive existence that identified human with their natural environment as a single entity. Through these cultural motifs, indigenous people in our region practice meaningful preservation and conservation of the biological diversity, which they formed a part of.

Another important practice of the Meitei people which symbolizes and exemplifies the deep concerns for the future generations is the ceremony called Ngamu Ushin Sinba [the sending forth ceremony of the Meitei Ngamu – Chana orientalis (Schenilder) – a small indigenous fish]. In this ceremony of ancient origin, fingerling sized Ngamu with two corns of rice (one red and one white) in their mouth are released into the water of rivers, ponds or other wetlands. The ceremony is performed during the month of Lamta (March-April) on a Saturday called *Lamtai Thangja*. By this sending forth ceremony, every individual member of the family hoped that they will be protected from all unfortunate circumstances during the ensuing year. This is yet another success story in the traditional conservation of biodiversity within an indigenous knowledge system, embedded as it is within a household cultural practice. The Ngamu is a very important fish, its flesh known to have great healing and invigorating powers, in the diet of the Meitei people. The fish is used during recuperation from illness, for the weaning of infants, for the elderly.

Among our indigenous people, there are important ceremonies and rituals associated with the felling of trees for various purposes. Among the Imemi (Mao people), there is an elaborate ritual that lasts several weeks before the felling of a great tree which is to be used to make the gate of the village – the *Koro*. Numerous such rituals are in existence among our people, before cutting bamboo, plantain, etc. and even before plucking the leaves of many plants. This shows an intimate relationship with the growing trees and plants. Many plants and trees are planted within the homestead lands by cultural norms and practices too. The people felt proud of their plants and flowers.

4

Inland Waters of Manipur Valley

Inland Waters

Inland waters are the repository of all terrestrial pollutants, as well as many airborne pollutants – all as a consequence of gravity. It is gravity and determines the flow of water down a stream or river. It is the same gravity that makes all soluble and small particulate matter moves inexorably towards the lowest point – the drainage of inland water, moving from gullies to streams and streams to rivers to lakes and swamps. Given such an obvious fact, inland waters can be viewed as systems under severe stress in relation to their water qualities and biodiversity components. Subsequently, aquatic organisms have a great disadvantage in relation to terrestrial types – they are unable to move without water of the right chemistry. Except in some exceptional cases, fish do not effectively traverse dry land, and more sensitive tax are even further restricted. In a state like Manipur where the areas of unpolluted inland waters are decreasing at an exponential rate, the ability of many species to survive is being lost. Correspondingly the life and culture of the indigenous population of the surrounding inland waters on wetland areas have been tremendously degraded. However, to testify the effects of acute problems of the inland water qualities of the Manipur valley is yet to be studied scientifically. In this context, it is urgently called for a co-coordinated and interdisciplinary effort of all concern involving the major stakeholders to save the wetlands of Manipur valley.

It may also be mentioned that dissolved solids, suspended particles of chemical pesticides, weedicides and fertilizers are of increasingly univocal. Loss of inland water endemic biodiversities and bio-resources becomes certain. For instance decrease of endemic fish fauna population may have correlations with increase in the pollution load in the inland waters of the Manipur valley. However, there is also a corresponding increase in the population of exotic fishes with an increase in pollution loads. The species of fish changed from natural to exotic as the ecosystems changed from clean to polluted ones. Thus, in a sense inland water systems are disproportionately rich and disproportionately imperiled. Inland waters are the critical link between landmass and the wetland, and virtually every human action is eventually reflected in them. Today, over 60% of the world's 5.6 billion people live within one kilometer of surface water. Given human dependence on their products and services, the loss of inland aquatic biodiversity has enormous ramifications.

Dramatic changes have been made to inland aquatic systems, and there have been dramatic declines in species and services. Twelve per cent of all animal species, including 41% of all recognized fish species, live in 1% of the earth's surface that is fresh water. At least 20% of the world's 9000 + fresh water fish species have become extinct, threatened, or endangered in recent years (Ranil Senanayake – 1997). The immediate causes of these losses include; habitat degradation; physical alteration of inland water systems; excessive withdrawal of water especially for power generation and irrigation; pollution; invasion by non-native species, and abuses of fisheries and its mismanagement.

Habitat Degradation

Human changes to the landscape are extensive and accelerating. Construction of Dams and surface road communication, flood control and irrigation structures are the most obvious signs of human intervention in the aquatic environment, but even in the absence of visible engineering works, the cumulative effects of human activities in the terrestrial landscape can be profound. Logging, mining, grazing, agriculture, industrialization, and urbanization – all these degrade inland waters and the lands they drain in ways that make them less able to support life and to provide valuable ecosystem services. For example, 80% of China's 50,000 km of major rivers no longer supports fish. In the same way the Imphal, the Iril and the Thoubal in Manipur valley are no longer supporting fish. Ultimately it may happen that the entire drainage system of Manipur may become devoid of many habitat types – such as wetlands, flood plains, waterfalls, and rapids – and the resident and migratory species adapted to those habitats.

Physical Modification

The extent of physical changes to inland water systems has increased tremendously during the last few decades. For example, the surface road construction (in between Uchiwa to Arong Nongmaikhong) cutting across the eastern portion of the Loktak Lake (1960s), surface road construction from Mayang Imphal to Thoubal across the Loktak Lake, Moirang-Sendra to Keibul Lamjao surface road connection across the Loktak Lake are the glittering examples of the physical modification of Loktak Lake. Construction of Dams and Barrages across the rivers of the Manipur valley viz., Sekmai, Imphal, Ithai, etc. are the best symptoms of physical modification of the Manipur valley have already been physically modified, reclaimed and encroached upon. Further, it may also be mentioned, herewith, that all the inland water bodies of the valley particularly Loktak and its associated lakes on the western side of the Manipur River and also other lakes of the eastern side of the Manipur River, namely Pumlen, Kharung, Khoidum, Ikop, etc. formed a wetland regime. Lakes of both sides of the Manipur River and its interfluves region together constitute the major inland water bodies or wetlands of the Manipur valley. These wetlands occupy about 419 sq. km. i.e. 21% of the Manipur valley area. The total drainage area of the Manipur River is the catchment areas of these wetlands. In a sense, these inland water bodies (wetlands) provide fundamental ecological functions including the regulation of water regime as well as providing habitats for flora and fauna of the region. Therefore, the wetlands of the Manipur valley provide globally significant social, economic and environmental benefits. However, the loss and degradation of inland waters in the valley of Manipur is driven by several factors. Increased demand of agricultural and piscicultural land associated with population growth and along with abuses of wetland resources continues to be a significant cause of wetland loss in the valley of Manipur. Infrastructure development and river flow regulation constitute another major cause of wetland degradation and loss, as well as the invasion of non-native species and pollution.

There has been little attention given so far by the State Planners and policy makers to the relationship between climate change and the conservation and wise use of the inland waters of the Manipur valley. Further, the State Authority needs to understand the varied components of inland water ecosystems which provide resources for direct human consumption including : water for drinking, fish, vegetable and fruit to eat, reeds for thatched roofs, peat and fuel for fire. It should also properly understand that the harvesting of inland water products, while respecting the production rate and the regenerative capacity of each species, can provide significant benefits to society. Over and above, wetland ecosystems also provide opportunities for recreation, aesthetic experience and reflection. Recreational uses include fishing, bird watching, photography, filming and water sports. Given that tourism is one of the leading income generating industries globally, the economic value of these can be considerably high. However, maintaining wetlands and capitalizing on these ecosystems. Therefore, generally we understood that the degradation and loss of wetland/inland water of the Manipur valley will certainly degrade and ultimately deprive us to those benefits and services.

The Way Forward

Virtually every part of the globe has lost fresh-water species and ecosystems, and none have escaped the cascade of unintended and unanticipated economic and social disruptions that follow the loss of healthy ecosystems, such as more frequent and devastating floods and droughts. Inland waters, along with their entire watershed and all their physical, chemical and biological elements, need to be viewed as part of a complex, integrated system of which human inhabitants are a part. In an ecosystem-based approach, resources can be managed over large enough areas and long enough time scale to allow their species and ecological processes to remain intact while still allowing human activity. On a social level, involving all stakeholders in defining problems, setting priorities and implementing solution is essential.

Our top priority is halting the further degradation of these systems. In places where the landscape has already been highly altered (like Loktak Lake, Loushi Pat, Poirou Pat) rehabilitation may be required, but it needs not be highly disruptive to existing uses and users of the landscape. For example, restoring just 50% of the wetlands lost in the Manipur River system will solve all the flood and drought problems of Manipur and also will be able to provide good quality drinking water to all sections of the people of Manipur.

Considering all these angles of consequences, every citizen of Manipur, particularly the major stakeholders of the inland waters of the valley, should make a coordinated effort for conserving and preserving the wetland resources for sustainable development and wise use of it. We may have a sincere approach for National heritage conservation particularly of wetland with the following concrete issues viz.,

1. The State should have water policy for sustainable and wise use of inland waters.
2. Demarcation of the wetland based on scientific definition and observation. For example, the State is still confused over the area of Loktak Lake. But on the other hand, Loktak Lake has already been included in the Ramsar List w.e.f. 23/03/90 in Ramsar Site No. 463 with an area of the Loktak Development Authority and the State Government to demarcate the area based on the Ramsar Site. After demarcating the lake area properly the State may construct a ring road around the Loktak Lake. No one should be allowed to encroach on the lake area inside the ring road. Simultaneously the State Authority should also initiate to include all the remaining inland water bodies and wetlands of the valley in the Ramsar list or take up immediate necessary actions for conservation and protection of these bodies for wise and sustainable uses.
3. All the catchment areas of the inland waters of the Manipur valley should be protected as per Law of Environment Protection Act etc.
4. There should be a system of interlinkage networking of different institutions and people who are in the field for the conservation, to ensure direct involvement of the masses.
5. There should be constant monitoring of the inland water ecosystem degradation and checking of water quality.

REFERENCES

Ramsar Convention on Wetlands.

1. *Biodiversity Bulletin* – 3 August 1997.
2. *The Annotated Ramsar List.*
3. *The Annotated Ramsar List:* India.
4. *Wetlands and Climate Change* – Background paper from IUCN, 1999.
5. Ramsar and Climate Change: report from Kyoto - 1977.

5

Climate Change and Its Impacts on Manipur River Systems

Background

Climate change, popularly known as global warming, has today become a major event of international negotiations. A Swedish chemistry scholar *Svante Arrhenius* described the basic mechanism underlying greenhouse gases (GHG) as early as 1896. The greenhouse effect is caused by the sun's radiation that is reflected off the earth's surface and trapped by carbon dioxide and other GHGs in the atmosphere. The natural greenhouse effect is beneficial for human and other biological sustenance. However, an abnormal emission of GHGs into the earth's atmosphere by burning fossil fuel and other anthropogenic activities is leading to the present stage of disastrous effects on the climate. The scenario of climate change and its impact on survival of species and other socio-economic dimensions are of extremes. According to the assessments of scientific body, the temperature rise of 1 to 3.5°C is expected due to global warming by 2100, the impact on the local and regional climates will very considerably. Its potential impacts are likely to include extreme weather conditions, greater intensity of floods and droughts, upsurge of diseases such as *malaria* and *dengue fever, asthma* and other respiratory illnesses due to global warming. Other possible impacts are habitat change and species extinction, adverse effects on agriculture due to changes in soil condition, water supply and water quality and change to mountain diversity and wetlands ecosystems. Here in this paper the author is trying to focus on the impacts of the localized issue in the state of Manipur.

Genesis of Manipur River System

The state of Manipur is located in the world's heaviest rainfall region and belongs to the catchment areas of two major drainage systems of the Asia's nine giant river systems i.e. the Brahmaputra-Barak and the Irrawaddy-Chindwin. These catchment area provides the natural flow to the rivers and the gravity helps them to flow into the valley of Manipur forming the cradle of diversified cultural heritage. They supply water for domestic consumption, hydropower forming lakes and wetlands allowing agricultural practices and also regulate the hydrological regime of the state. During the rain mountain and its forest cover allow to absorb the rain water and percolate down to the aquifer layers for enriching the ground water table.

Manipur, because of its peculiar geographic situation in the *Indo-Myanmar Arc* system and watershed areas of the Manipur River Basin (one of the major headstreams of the Irrawaddy-Chindwin River System of Burma), is blessed with an enormously rich diverse heritage of *riverine ecosystem*. Wetlands of the Manipur Valley are popularly known by the generic name *Pat* while rivers are known as *Turels*. In addition to the lavish natural endowment of this State, indigenous population have also built up a highly sophisticated and endemic engineering marvel that extends the wetlands, and their benefits – the traditional drainage and flood control system of *Khongs, Khongbals* and artificially developed *Turels*.

The probable genesis of the valley of Manipur seems to be caused by tectonic disturbances in the course of the Manipur River near *Serou*. This area is popularly known as *Sugnu Hump*. In fact, the emergence of Sugnu Hump affected not only the normal flow of the Manipur River but also contributed to develop a delicate balance between the normal rate of erosion of the river and depth of the river bed. It is, precisely for the reason that this portion of the Manipur River is termed as *antecedent drainage* by the geomorphologist. The flow of the Manipur River declined near the Sugnu Hump as the level of the river bed rose up. Consequently, during the monsoon, immense volume of water use to get accumulated and impounded upward to form a vast sheet of water. However, in course of time, the level of water receded and formed the valley of Manipur with a number of lakes and wetlands. During the processes of valley formation, there were a huge number of wetlands and lakes, geo-strategically located in between the interfluves areas of different tributaries of the Manipur River system. Thus, the valley of Manipur exists due to a delicate balance between the rate of upliftment and down cutting by Manipur River. Geological evidences also proved that the Manipur River existed before the land in the south Manipur Hills underwent upliftment (*Geographical Review of India,* Vol. 44, No. Dec. 1982).

The drainage networking systems of Manipur state may be grouped into two viz., (1) the Irrawaddy-Chindwin system and (2) the Barak system.

(1) The Manipur River system is one of the main head streams of the Chindwin River of Burma. The eastern half of the State has been predominantly drained by the Manipur River and its tributaries. This system consists of two sub-groups of tributaries i.e. (i) tributaries directly discharging to the Manipur River and (ii) those tributaries directly discharging into the Loktak Lake (Ramsar Site) and other wetlands of the Manipur Valley. Imphal, Iril, Thoubal, Sekmaijin, Khuga and Chakpi belong to the first sub-group, while Nambul, Nambol. Thongjaorok, Ningthoukhong, Yangoi Achouba and Macha, Moirang and other 4 or 5 rivulets and streams with a combined discharge basin of about 650 sq. km. flow into the Loktak

Lake. It is interesting to note that channels of Khordak and Ungamel emerge from the Loktak Lake and joins the Manipur River, which is so far fed by the first sub-group of the tributaries. From the points of confluences of the Khordak and the Ungamel with the Manipur River the single river system commanding almost whole of Manipur emerges.

The long profile of the Manipur River shows that it runs through a smooth gradient from its origin in the north (Ukhrul and part of Senapati districts of Manipur State) down to the Imphal City. In this part the Manipur River is known as Iril River. The Imphal and the Iril – these two big rivers of the valley meet at Lillong Township. From the confluence of the Iril and the Imphal upward the total length of the Iril is 120 km and that of the Imphal is 75 km. The Thoubal River joins the main river near Mayang Imphal Township. It has a total length of 105 km. All these three rivers have a combine catechment area of about 2,600 sq.km. The Thoubal River has a steep gradient and brings a huge load of sediments and debris to the Valley of Manipur. As a result the floodplain area of the Thoubal River is one of the most fertile paddy fields of the State. Further south, the Manipur River receives another two of its big tributaries coming from the opposite direction i.e. from the southern direction. The Khuga River meets it near Ethai. The river has a course of 80 km and drainage basin of about 620 sq. km. and the Chakpi River (meets the Manipur River near Sugnu Township with a course length of 60 km and commands a drainage basin of about 800 sq. km) being mountainous streams of steep gradient, during the monsoon, brought a huge volume of water along with coarse sediments that block the normal flow of the Manipur River temporarily. Although the level of the Manipur River bed is lower than that of the Loktak water level, yet during the monsoon flood, the huge impounded water of the Manipur River is flowing into the Loktak Lake through the Khordak channel. When the monsoon water of the Khuga and the Chakpi rivers recedes then the Manipuri River reclaims its southwards flow of the excess water of the Loktak Lake. Thus, the Khordak acts as a communication channel in between the Manipur River and the Loktak Lake. However, the Ungamel channel drained out only the excess water of the Loktak Lake by joining the Manipur River near the confluence point of the Khuga and the Manipur River. On the other hand, the Loktak Lake acts as a temporary natural reservoir of the excess monsoon water like that of the Tole Sap of Kampuchea (Cambodia) which acts as a temporary water reservoir for the flood water of the Mekong River. After the confluence of the Chakpi River, the Manipur River flows pass through a long deep gorge and finally joined the Chindwin River below the Kalemyo Town of Upper Burma. Basically Manipur River flows through the valley of Manipur and form a regime of wetland complex.

(2) The Barak River system consists of five main tributaries namely, Barak, Makru, Irang, Tuivai and Jiri Rivers. The Barak, Makru, Irang and Jiri originated from the southern slopes of the western Manipur mountain ranges while Tuivai, has its origin in Burma and joined by the Tuila, Tuilak and Tuisa Rivers before the confluence with the Barak at Tipaimukh (the proposed controversial Tipaimukh High Dam site).

In the distant past, the Manipur River system promotes and influenced the existence of varied biodiversity along with endemism species of flora and fauna and durable climatic condition in the valley of Manipur. What now remains of the once rich valley of Manipur is like the skeleton of a sick man, all the fat and soft earth having wasted away, only the bare framework is left. Formerly, many of the wetlands in the valley and fountain, springs and waterfalls in the catchments areas of the Manipur River were luxuriant with varieties of bio-resources. Moreover, the whole river basin was enriched by monsoon rains, which were not lost, as now, but excessive surface runoff causing soil erosion in the catchment area and siltation to the river beds and valley wetlands. Further, if there be a continuous widespread raining for three days in the catchment areas of the Manipur River there will be flash floods in the valley of Manipur. It is observed that the monsoon system has also globally turns towards an abnormal character. As a result Manipur has been experiencing a trend of occurrence of frequent floods and droughts in the same year for the last two decades. This year we are experiencing heavy rainfall during the months of January and February while in the year 2007 the state was affected by floods twice alternately within three months. During winter this year, the state faced the experience of cold waves and temperature below 4°C continuously during the last week of January to the second week of February. Hence unpredictable weather conditions caused by the climate change is experiencing in the state of Manipur.

Developmental Interventions in Manipur and Climate Change

The ecological integrity and biological diversity of Manipur and other North East parts of the country are subjected to climate changes on account of aggressive and unsustainable developmental initiatives, ranging from construction of mega dams, indiscriminate logging, other extractive industry, carbon-emitting industries, urbanization etc. Climate change had caused massive loss of lives, species extinction, undermined food sovereignty, intensified floods, water shortages etc. Indigenous and tribal communities, impoverished rural communities and especially women and children are the most vulnerable to these negative impacts. The introduction of these development projects is amidst absence of taking thorough consideration and assessment of holistic impact assessments and also primarily without respecting and adhering to established norms of free, prior and informed consent that ensures participation of indigenous people in decision making processes on developmental initiatives affecting their land and resources.

Manipur has already been subjected to introduction and implementation of massive unsustainable developmental initiatives, with primary contributions to climate change. The Loktak Multipurpose Hydro Electric Power Project, the Tipaimukh Multipurpose Hydroelectric Project, the Khoupum Dam, the Thoubal Multipurpose Hydroelectric Project, Khuga Multipurpose Project, the Dolaithabi Barrage, the Sekmai Barrage are some of the mega project interventions on wetlands and rivers of Manipur.

The Ithai Barrage of the Loktak Multipurpose Project on the Manipur River, constructed in 1979 and commissioned in 1984, and with power generating capacity of 105 MW (3 x 35 MW), has 'permanently' raised the water level of Loktak and its adjoining wetlands and has blocked the natural flow of water to and or from the wetland, severely altering the hydrologic cycle of a delicately balanced system of Manipur Valley. Before the construction of the Ithai Barrage, the natural dredging process continuously cleared the silt brought down by various streams and rivers from the valley and the hills. The main reasons behind steady deterioration in the condition of the Loktak Lake since the commissioning of the Ithai Barrage and already acknowledged by the Ramsar Wetlands International Secretariat includes the commissioning of the Loktak Hydro Electric Project, drying up the beds of the rivers which fall into Loktak.

Notwithstanding the implications of the Loktak Multipurpose Project and its contribution to climate change, the state is planning for a series of mega project interventions, further impacting the delicate hydrological balance of Manipur. The proposed Tipaimukh, that will be constructed 500 m downstream from the confluence of the Barak and the Tuivai Rivers in the southwestern corner of Manipur (24°14'N and 93°1.3'E approximately) will permanently submerge an area of 275.50 sq. km. in the state of Manipur. A large number of people, mostly belonging to the Zeliangrong and Hmar tribes, will be displaced permanently and deprived them of the rights to their environment and to their age-old traditional occupations. Official figures state that 1,461 Hmar families will be directly displaced due to the project. The River Barak is the second largest drainage system in northeast India. The project envisions a 390 m long 162.8 m high earthen-rock filled dam across the Barak, 500 m downstream of the confluence of the Tuivai and the Barak on the Manipur-Mizoram border. The dam, that will be constructed at an altitude of about 180 m above mean sea level with a maximum reservoir level of 178 m and with installation capacity of 6 x 250 =1500 MW and a firm generation of 412 MW, will further contribute in ever visible climate change implications in Manipur and other parts of India'a Northeast.

It is a well-known fact that the construction of dams invariably destroys the natural riverine ecosystem. As a result, it affects the habitat of rare and endemic species of flora and fauna. Construction of a high dam disturbs river functions, causes floods, dries out downstream flood plains, devastates riverside ecology, obstructs the migratory path of fish and other aquatic fauna, prevents the exchange of micro-nutrients and silt between the upper and lower reaches of river and has an overall adverse affect on the riverine food chain.

Way Forward

Unfortunately, many of the projects, projected as CDM projects, primarily the Hydel project in India's North-east will be located on lands of the indigenous and highlanders, where their intrinsic and traditional rights over their land, their rivers, forest and rights surrounding such relationships have not been recognized. The social, cultural, health implications on indigenous people in terms of displacement, loss of livelihood and destruction of culture and traditional institutions is not considered while introducing such (un) sustainable initiatives.

A new approach of modern developmental planning should always try to define a specific zone or region for effective and holistic planning, primarily for interventions on river basins. River basin is a *geographical unit* enclosing an area drained by streams and channels that feed a river at a particular area. All the precipitation that falls on these slopes will either evaporate, used by plants and other living organisms sink into the ground or end up in the river after various natural and man-made uses. Thus, it follows that river basin provides an important region to understand the implication of any particular form of human use of water. Development agencies and institutions need to promote realistic options for basin development and provide a flexible framework for managing the complex and dynamic river basin system. A holistic developmental approach in the entire river basin of Manipur should be taken up to enable the region to grow in a self-reliant and sustainable manner. Informed participation from all sections of the population in the decision-making process is imperative to arrive at decisions that are sustainable and socially just. The implications of CDM projects on climate change and subsequent livelihood and survival issues of the people should be well addressed. Such a basin-wide approach will enable us to gain a better understanding of the ecosystem functions, values and requirements and how community livelihoods depend on and influence them. Such an understanding will be crucial to ensure that the energy, water infrastructure development to meet local needs is sensitive to the social and ecological values of the region.

As indigenous people and highlanders live in sensitive zones where effects of climate change are most devastating and where traditional ways of life are disproportionately affected by climate change particularly in forest, wetland, river, all developmental models should be premised on respecting the collective right to a pattern of development that is fundamentally of the choice of the people, the right for them to decide their way of development.

The rights to full and prior information and consent regarding all development conservation or other policy initiatives and planning and full transparency in all CDM projects should be respected. The initiatives should also be undertaken in a culturally and linguistically appropriate manners, ensure respect and full adherence of the principles and practices of transparency, monitoring, benefit sharing, risk reduction, appeals mechanisms etc.

6

Mountain Biodiversity of Manipur

> "Mountain might seem like impenetrable monoliths of rock but, in reality, they are among the world's greatest sources of biodiversity, providing refuge to untold varieties of plants and animals. Many of these species have disappeared from lowland areas, crowded out by human activities. Many other exist nowhere else but on mountains. All people, wherever they like, share the responsibility of protecting mountain biodiversity. But it is mountain people who are the primary guardians of these irreplaceable global assets. Over generations, they have acquired a unique and detailed understanding of mountain ecosystems. Until now, governments and international organizations have largely overlooked the knowledge that mountain people possess and the important role that mountains play in preserving much of the world's biodiversity". (International Year of Mountain IYM – 2002)

Background

Mountains have been described as islands of biodiversity surrounded by an ocean of monocultures and human-altered landscapes. Indeed, varieties of flora and fauna species found in mountain habitat have disappeared from plains and lowland regions, crowd out by human activities. Today, mountain covers only about 25% of the Earth's surface and are home to about 12% of the human population. They host a significant component of the world's biodiversity and many of the food staples on which humans depend originated in mountain ecosystem (IUCN).

Slope and ruggedness of the terrain, together with absolute altitude, determine many of the fundamental characteristics of mountain environments. Position on the Earth's surface imposes further diversity on these basic features, primarily through the effects of latitude and continentally on climate and local weather patterns, so that some mountains are almost permanently wet, other dry and other highly seasonal. Geological substrate adds a further dimension on diversity by influencing the soil type and the potential erosion.

The vegetation zones encountered with increasing elevation on an idealized tropical mountain tend to resemble the biome types found with increasing latitude. Vegetation types similar to those that succeed one another through more than 80% of latitude and 3000 km distance – tropical moist, deciduous forest, coniferous forest, shrub and grassland, or ice – may be compressed onto the slopes of a mountain perhaps 5000 m high.

About 10% of the world's population depends directly on the use of mountain resources for their livelihoods and well-being, and an estimated 40% depends indirectly on them for water, hydroelectricity, timber, mineral resources, recreation and flood control. Mountains are the earth's unique freshwater reservoirs. They store immense amounts of water and hold them to gradually release to support the lives downstream [International Centre for Integrated Mountain Development (ICIMOD)]. Despite their critical importance for the well-being of humanity, mountains receive little attention in the international development agenda.

Globalization as an economic, trade, finance, and communication phenomenon is well-recognized and even those questioning it tend to agree that globalization cannot be stopped. We might be economically globalized, but on the other hand we are culturally becoming more and more local. We value local products, appreciate an ecologically intact landscape, we have sympathies for local difference, we celebrate them! This also refers to the ethnic aspects and has led to excesses in areas where the state had completely imploded and where ethnic identification has been questioned and associated with scared resources. Thus, globalization has created localization. In this context, mountains have become a space for retreat, for recovery, and for identification.

Globalization and climate change have brought other dimensions to the awareness of the scientists, environmentalists, and a growing number of citizens and politicians. The vision of melting glaciers and of mountains falling down because of receding permafrost has become a frightening vision. Mountains were building for eternity and the growing concern for the system of sustainability. This refers to the familiar panorama of snowcapped mountains, the wealth of biodiversity as a source of beauty and recovery, but also as a heritage for mankind. In its reality the availability of water, electricity, reaches the basic requirements and services we need for our survival. All of a sudden, mountains as a natural system with natural and human features are not anymore in a position to provide the services we have taken for granted (ICIMOD). With this background the present status of Manipur Mountains may be observed as hereunder.

Manipur

The mountain landscapes of Manipur have fashioned an equally fascinating array of human cultures, sensitively interplay with the intrinsic rhythms of nature: the inexorable pulsations of the earth below, tempered by the elements above. The mountain ranges of Manipur occupy 80% of the total surface area of the State and are home of the 29 sub-tribes of the Tibeto-Mongoloid group. In a sense, the

State of Manipur may be described as a mountainous State. These mountains have significant ecological, aesthetic, and socioeconomic importance not only for those highlanders but also for the people living beyond. Till today the mountains of Manipur are the home to indigenous highlanders with varied cultures, values, dialects, and indigenous knowledge systems. This remarkable socioeconomic and cultural diversity is matched by a high degree of environmental diversity with huge variations in climate, soil, vegetation, and wildlife within the region. Isolation a relatively inaccessible in the recent past have helped in protecting and preserving the endemic species in the mountain ranges of Manipur. There are more than hundreds of rice cultivars, medicinal plants and herbs are still productively cultivated and use by the highlander. These precious reserves of genetic diversity are our insurance for the future, particularly as the global economy continues to turn lowland habitats into fields of high-yielding food crops – monocultures that feed the ever increasing demands of the growing population of the state but are vulnerable to evolving pest and pathogens.

Because of their shape and size, the mountains of Manipur support a wide range of micro-climate zones. Climbing just 50 m up on the mountain slope of Manipur you will be able to experience of as much as climatic variety as traveling of 50 km across flat terrain. The micro-climate zones of the Manipur Mountains are like narrow bands, each stacked on top of the other. Every rise in altitude generates different conditions, supporting unique and often isolated ecosystems with some of the world's greatest variety of plant and animal life. Much of the North East's remaining native biological diversity especially of species and ecosystems is in the mountains of Manipur. Great diversity of endemism is largely due to the extreme heterogeneity of environment (micro-climate and soils) because of the rapid altitudinal changes (altitudinal vegetation belts), and abundant micro-habitats.

The mountains of Manipur are located in the heaviest rainfall region of the world and belongs to the catchment areas of two major drainage systems of Asia's nine giant river systems i.e. the Brahmaputra-Barak and the Irrawaddy-Chindwin. These catchment areas provide the natural flow to the rivers and the gravity helps them to flow into the valley of Manipur forming the cradle of diversified cultural heritage. They supply water for domestic consumption, hydropower, forming lakes and wetlands allowing agricultural practices and also regulate the hydrological regime of the state. During the rain mountain and its forest cover allow to be absorbed the rain water and percolate down to the aquifer layers for enriching the ground water table. In a sense, the mountains of Manipur are outflow areas, where not only physical mountain products soil, fuel wood, timber, minerals, agricultural products, game, non-wood forest products move down slope to the valley, even young and educated people were migrated downwards to the valley as a flow out.

The earth's climate has been changing after being warm through much of history over the last 130 million years. Increasing CO_2 emissions in the atmosphere generated by human activities since the Industrial Revolution, and particularly since the 1960s, has thus led to increase in the earth's mean global temperature. The present phenomenon of global climate change, the conditions within each of these narrow bands of micro-climatic zones are also changing. Already scientists (IYM – 2002) have witnessed examples of species moving uphill in search of more suitable habitat. Further, climatologists also believe that a predicted rise in global temperatures of 3¼C would be equivalent to an ecological shift upwards of about 500 m in altitude. Those confined to the tops of mountains or below impassable barriers may face extinction as their habitat grows smaller. These similar kinds of syndromes are visible at the peaks of Mt. Koubru, Mt. Esso, Mt. Khongho, Mt. Godai and Mt. Siroi etc. the rarest species are most at risk of extinction.

Among those species, high-altitude butterflies may be mentioned herewith.

Healthy mountain forests are crucial to the ecological health of the state of Manipur. They protected watersheds and supply fresh water to all over the State and more particularly to the Valley of Manipur. They also harbour untold number a wildlife, provide food and fodder for the inhabitants. In the last decade, mountain forests have been disappearing at an astounding rate. Deforestation, while a complex phenomenon is generally driven by population growth, unstable urbanization and its unplanned extension of infrastructural development. After centuries of population growth and intensive land use, mountain forests have been reduced to small patch of green. Ongoing agricultural practices are unsuitable and contribute to deforestation and accelerate hillside erosion, threatening mountain biodiversity and impairing the natural processes of forest ecosystems. Indeed, the destabilization of mountain forests creates an ever-escalating spiral of destruction. For example, when too many trees are cut, run off and soil erosion increase at rates 20 to 40 times faster than soil can be stabilized, impairing water quality in streams and rivers and harming fish and other aquatic species.

Human activities like endless abuse and misuse of mountain slopes and forests clubbed with the current trend of global climate change are profoundly degrading the mountain biodiversity of Manipur. As the slopes of the mountains were endlessly and recklessly deforested by different anthropogenic activities causing mass soil wash on the slopes of the mountains while the river beds and wetlands in the valley were silted with the debris brought down from the mountain. At the same time mountains of Manipur will become more dangerous as the surface runoff accelerate soil erosion as well as mudflows in places like Gopibung, landslides along the national Highways i.e. 39 and 53 and frequent flash floods in the Valley. As a result, the state of Manipur will be affected, first by frequent flash floods and then by drought making harder and harder economic activities both in the mountain regions and the valley of Manipur. Natural resources and accompanying environmental and ecosystem services and increasingly degraded. The natural processes of change, always mercifully slow enough in the recent past to enable a creative reordering of human activities have, over the past decades of radically new techno-economic structures, acquired a speed that threatens to destabilize many critical subsystems of biodiversity in the state mountain. The most serious result is an almost irreversible erosion of the regenerate capacity of vital ecological niches crucial for the sustenance of the mountain communities. Today, increasing demand and advances in technology have made even the most remote mountain areas accessible and profitable for logging, fuel-wood, charcoal and mining. These activities may bring large benefits to the mountain communities, but it can also be devastating to fragile mountain ecosystems, mountain cultures and environments.

Secondly, mountain-dwellers cultivate thousands of varieties, of crops and plants many of which thrive only at specific elevations and micro-climatic zones. However, with the pressure of market economy and urbanization processes, they encourage cross-fertilization between wild and cultivated varieties. In the districts of Ukhrul and Tamenglong, domestic and wild varieties of lemon, orange and plantains are grown side by side. Varieties of vegetables, fruits, other HYV crops and flowers were introduced and cultivated popularly in Senapati and Ukhrul districts. Sometimes mountain ecosystems have no naturally evolved defenses against invading species. Often, these alien invaders are introduced by human visitors or as a consequence of planting non-native crops or ornamental plants. Under such circumstances varieties of native flora and fauna were completely extinct and some are on the verge of extinction from the mountains of Manipur. To save the situation, mountain-friendly policies and laws are vital to protect mountain ecosystem and support mountain people. Generally individual mountain dwellers do not have land ownership right. In many cases, mountain resources fall under the village authorities and Chief of the village. Policies and laws that recognize individual property right are essential for sustainable mountain development.

Lastly, mountains of Manipur are the barometer of climate change in the region. These fragile ecosystems are highly sensitive to changes in temperature and variation on precipitations. Indeed, many climatologists believe mountains provide an early glimpse of what may come to pass in lowland or valley environments. For this reason, it is vital that the biological and physical components of the mountains of Manipur are strictly monitored and studied. The research and project works conducted by the department of Life Sciences and the Earth Sciences of Manipur University may be mentioned as the initial ground work and documentation for conserving the mountain biodiversity of Manipur. However, it is high time to establish a Department of Mountain Science in the University to study and for monitoring the biodiversity and the physical component of the mountains of Manipur.

REFERENCES

1. Rhoades, R.E. 1985, *Farming on high in: Mountain Peoples,* Ed. By M. Tobias. Norman University of Oklahoma Press, pp. 39-44.
2. Bernbaum, E. 1992, *Sacred Mountains of the World*, Sierra Club Books.
3. Kapas, V., Rhind, J., Edwards, M., *Developing a Map of the World's Mountain Forests,* CAB International, Wallingford: 49.
4. Meybeck, M. Green, P and Vorosmarty, C. 2001 *A New Typology for Mountains and Other Relief Classes. An Application to Global Continental Water Resources and Population Distribution.* Mountain Research and Development. Vol. 21 (I): 34-45.
5. *Mountain Biodiversity: An Introduction for the International Year of Mountains,* 2002.

6. Sustainable Mountain Development in the Greater Himalayan Region, No. 53, Winter 2007, International Centre for Integrated Mountain Development, pp. 5-17.
7. IUCN, The World Conservation Union, *Annual Report (Asia Region – 2006)*.
8. Jim Thorsell, Larry Hamilton, 2002, *A Global Overview of Mountain Protected Areas on the World Heritage List.*
9. UNESCO, 2007, *Case Studies on Climate Change and World Heritage*, France.

7

Changing Land Use Pattern in the Hills of Manipur: Its Impact on Biodiversity

Introduction

Manipur is a state of the North East India, geographically located in a zone where the world's heaviest rainfall is received. It has an area of 22,327 square kilometer, stretching in between the gradients of 92°58'E to 94°45'E longitudes and 23°50'N to 25°42'N latitudes with a population of 2,293,896 persons. The State has a total boundary line of about 854 km in length of which 353 km in length falls under the jurisdictions of International boundary line in between Burma (Myanmar) and India. The remaining 501 km in length boundary lines are with the neighbouring states of Nagaland in the North, Cachar District of Assam in the West and Mizoram in the South and Southwest. The state of Manipur is occupying an area of 0.68 per cent of the total geographical area of the country and 20th place in the aerial spread in the country. It is a landlocked isolated hilly state having a distinct geographical entity. It is almost rectangular in shape with a valley encircled by hilly ranges of Indo-Burma Arc. The average elevation of the valley is 790 m above mean sea level with a gradient from north to south. The hill ranges are spread parallel from north to south direction with an average height ranging between 1,500 to 1,800 m. Some of the peaks like the Mt. Esso have a height around 3000m above sea level.

The state of Manipur is drained by two major drainage systems of the Asia's nine giant river systems i.e. the Brahmaputra-Barak Basin and the Irrawaddy-Chindwin Basin. The Barak sub-basin originates from the hill complex of Lai-Leeyai, Senapati District and drained the western half of Manipur. The Barak sub-system consists of five main tributaries namely, Barak, Makru, Irang, Tuivai and Jiri rivers. Although the main Chindwin basin falls within the territory of Burma, a large number of its headstreams drain the eastern part of Manipur. The Manipur River sub-basin includes the tributaries Iril, Imphal, Thoubal, Sekmaijin, Khurga, Chakpi and the Loktak bound rivers etc. Catchment areas of these two sub-basins spread all over the sub-tropical monsoon to temperate areas of the five hill districts of Manipur. It has an annual average rainfall ranging from 1016 to 1778 mm.

Catchment areas of the above mentioned two sub-basins of the Barak and the Manipur River are inhabited by the indigenous highland communities with their age old traditional practices of Shifting cultivation or Jhum cultivation as predominant land use system. Shifting cultivation is an old topic, and there is plenty of conventional wisdom, set opinions, and policies that have been in place for a long time. It has been generally and widely considered that shifting cultivation is always not favoured from both environmental and socioeconomic perspectives. However, shifting cultivation is the most prominent farming system, providing a way of life for almost all the entire population of the highland communities in the state. Jhumming is characterized by a short 'cultivation phase' of a few years followed by a relatively longer 'forestry phase' usually referred to as the 'fallow'.

Changing Land Use Pattern

The long-term effects of changes in land use and land cover on human welfare and physical environment may be as significant, if not more so, than those associated with the climate change. Unlike global warming, however, land use and land cover changes are undisputed aspects of global environmental change. These changes and their impacts are with us now, ranging from potential climate warming to land degradation and biodiversity loss and food production to spread of infectious disease.[1] There is no systematic record on land use and land cover change or about the prevailing land use practices and land tenure systems of the ethnic highlanders that inhabit in the hills of Manipur. But it is a fact that all the hill areas of Manipur has been predominantly under the practice of shifting or jhumming cultivation for centuries, if not millennia. However, general land use studies of the state are being carried out based on topographic maps, field visit, aerial photography and application of remote sensing techniques. Land resources of the state of Manipur are given below Table 1.

TABLE 1

Land Resources of Manipur (1980)

Sl. No.	*Category*	*Area (in sq. kms)*	*Percentage to State Geographical Area*
1	Forest	15,154.00	67.0
2	Agricultural	338.04	1.5
3	Crop Land	3,170.72	14.2
4	Pasture & Barren	1,539.03	6.9
5	Urban Sites	293.13	1.3
6	Current Jhum	1,832.08	8.3
	Total	22,327.00	99.2

Source: Forest Department, Government of Manipur, 1997.

The paper reviewed the available land use data recorded by different departments of the state Government. The State Revenue Department notified 15,154 sq. km of area as forest which represent 67.87 per cent of the state total geographical area. This area has further been classified as i) Reserved Forest (1,463 km^2 i.e. 6.55%); ii) Protected Forest (4,171 km^2 i.e. 18.68%) and iii) Unclassed forest

(9,520 km^2 i.e. 42.62%). All these forest areas are owned by the Department of Forest, Government of Manipur. Further, area under forests includes all lands classed as forests under any legal enactment dealing with forests or administered as forests whether State owned or private and wooded or maintained as potential forest land. The area of crops raised in the forests and grazing lands or area open for grazing within the forests are generally included under the forest area. The land use and land coverage area of the state, in the year 1989-90, the area under land with or without forest also included (Table 2).

TABLE 2

Land Use Classes in the Hill Forest Areas of the State

Sl. No.	*Land use classes*	*Area in sq. km.*	*Percentage*
1.	Dense tree forests	451.4	2.98
2.	Moderately dense tree forests	5182.99	32.2
3.	Open tree forests	1684.67	11.12
4.	Scrub forests	338.55	2.23
5.	Bamboo brakes	1587.95	10.48
6.	Shifting cultivation	1370.31	9.04
7.	Plantation	1362.25	9.00
8.	Grass lands	96.73	0.64
9.	Agri. land without tree	137.03	0.90
10.	Agri. land with tree	161.21	1.06
11.	Non-forestry plantation	8.06	0.05
12.	Habitation	145.09	0.96
13.	Water bodies	32.24	0.21
14.	Young crops	959.22	6.33
15.	Inaccessible	1636.30	10.8
	Total	15154.00	98%

Interestingly, it is also observed that different state departments have maintained different data with different classifications of the land use and land coverage of the state (Table: 2 & 3). Based on these figures and classifications no systematic analysis and interpretation is possible. Further, it is also observed that the State Forest Department shows the increased areas of forest coverage in the state by manipulating the universal convention on land use and land classification codification.

TABLE 3

Land Use and Land Cover of Manipur 1989-90

Sl. No.	*Category*	*Area in hectare*	*Percentage to the total Area*
1.	Settlement	545.20	2.48
2.	Agricultural	1485.72	6.66
3.	Forest:		
	(i) Dense Forest	1019.90	4.57
	(ii) Moderate Forest	9975.99	44.64
	(iii) Land with or without scrub*	8646.12	38.72
4.	Water bodies	707.79	2.93
	Total		22380.72
100.00			

* It includes Jhumming, terrace and plantation area.

Source: State Remote Sensing Centre, DSTE, Government of Manipur, 1990.

Here the author reviewed all the available published data of the different State departments and observed the increasing trend of deforestation in the hills of Manipur. Subsequently, land under tree crops, cultivable waste, and land put to nonagricultural and permanent pasture and grazing land areas were in the increasing trends. Further, integrated with the development of spatial database and information collected through interview with jhummias and other key informants and analysis of relevant socio-economic policies. The spatial databases served as a framework for analyzing changes in land use and forest coverage patterns in the hills of Manipur. These spatial databases were developed using toposheets, maps as well as Landsat TM and IRS ID L3 images. Table 4 shows the increasing trend of shifting cultivation areas (Jhumming) during the year 1988 and 2003.

TABLE 4

Shifting Cultivation in Manipur Districts *(Area in Sq. Km)*

Districts	*1988*	*1998*	*2000*	*2003*
Churachandpur	166.78	101.61	265.16	289.10
Chandel	176.70	106.95	139.21	228.98
Senapati	65.09	55.22	56.15	34.01
Tamenglong	147.45	87.66	263.89	43.08
Ukhrul	184.94	143.74	193.70	164.40

Source: Landsat TM, IRS-1D L3 imageries.

Jhumming (shifting cultivation) and its associated stages of secondary vegetation pose particular problems for monitoring because they are not captured well in traditional land-cover classes of agriculture, plantation, forest, etc. Brookfield and Byron[2] suggest that as much as 26% of all land in Southeast Asia can be classified as "other" where other is defined as shrub, brush, pasture, waste and other land-use categories, many of which are actually secondary and tertiary vegetation.

Healthy forest coverage in hills is crucial to the ecological health of the state of Manipur. They protected watersheds and supply fresh water to all over the State and more particularly to the Valley of Manipur. They also harbor untold wildlife, provide food and fodder for the inhabitants. In the last decade, mountain forests have been disappearing at an astounding rate. Deforestation, a complex phenomenon, is generally driven by population growth, unstable urbanization and its unplanned extension of infrastructural development. After centuries of population growth and unsuitable land use practices the forest coverage in the hills has been reduced to small patch of green. Ongoing agricultural practices are unsuitable and contribute to deforestation which accelerates hillside erosion, threatening mountain biodiversity and impairing the natural processes of forest ecosystems. Indeed, the destabilization of forest coverage creates an ever-escalating spiral of destruction. For example, when too many trees are cut, runoff and soil erosion increase at rates 20-40 times faster than what the soil can be stabilized, impairing water quality in streams and rivers and harming fish and other aquatic species.

Human activities like endless abuse and misuse of hill slopes and forests clubbed with the current trend of global climate change are profoundly degrading the mountain biodiversity of Manipur. As the slopes of the hills were endlessly and recklessly deforested by different anthropogenic activities causing Mass soil wash on the slopes of the mountains while the river beds and wetlands in the valley were silted with the debris brought down from the hilly ranges. As a result, the state of Manipur will be affected, first by frequent flash floods and then by drought making harder and harder economic activities both in the hilly regions and the valley of Manipur. Natural resources and accompanying environmental and ecosystem services are increasingly degraded. Further it is also reported that more than 900 sq.km of forested areas in the hill has been transformed into jhum fields annually (Department of Forest). Consequent upon the unchecked increasing trend of population growth on the limited hill areas of Manipur, the Jhum Cycle has been shortened from 20-30 years to 2-3 years. The natural processes of change, always mercifully slow enough in the recent past to enable a creative reordering of human activities have, over the past decades of radically new techno-economic structures, acquired a speed that threatens to destabilize many critical subsystems of biodiversity in the hills of the state. The most serious result is an almost irreversible erosion of the regenerative capacity of vital ecological niches crucial for the sustenance of the highland communities. Today, increasing demand and advances in technology have made even the most remote hilly regions accessible and profitable for logging, fuel-wood and mining. These activities may bring large economic benefits to the highland communities, but it can also be devastating to fragile highland ecosystems, highland cultures and environments.

REFERENCES

1. LUCC International Project Office Page. *The International Gesophere-Biosphere Programmed.* 1 January 1999. (ww.icc.es/lucc/what is lucc/what is html).
2. L. Potter, H. Brookfield, Y. Byron (1994): *The Sundaland Region of Southeast Asia.* In J. Kasperson, R. Kasperson, B. Turner II (Eds) *Regions at Risk: Comparison on Threatened Environments.* Tokyo: United Nations University Press.
3. *Economic Review 1990-91,* Directorate of Economic & Statistics, Government of Manipur, Imphal, p. 35 (Table-30).
4. Agricultural Census Report of Manipur, 1976-77, Department of Agriculture, Government of Manipur, p. 18 (Table 8).

8

Traditional System of Preserving Ecosystem in Manipur

Conceptualization

The dawning of new century has throughout history been as an appropriate time to reflect on the one hundred years that have gone before and, if necessary, to chart a new cause for the future. As we are privileged to be standing on the threshold of both a new century and millennium, such reflection seems especially the right time.

This is particularly so when one looks at the state of the natural environment. While the environment continues to be seen in some circles as peripheral, a 'side' issue as it were, there is an increasing recognition that it is in fact "the context of everything else", and that humans are inseparable from the ecosystems in which they live. Rapidly declining biological diversity, increased evidence of climate change, ongoing deforestation etc. is some of the bleaker indicators. Environmental degradation often has the greatest impact on the world's poorest people, who depend directly on their environment for food, drinking water, shelter etc. and often experience the severest effects of environmental pollution. Subsequently, the impact of environmental degradation on future generation is also of great concern. "The responsibility of the present generation is to ensure that future generations will have the freedom to sustain their lives on this planet" (Annan: 2000).

The causes of this very serious state of environmental affairs are complex. One of the most important factors is that the earth's ecosystems and how they function have been continued to be taken for granted in humankind's pursuit of economic growth. As a result, present systems of production and consumption, and the governance structures which preside over them, are both fundamentally out of touch with the interconnected and cyclical patterns of the natural world and unable to adapt to change in these patterns.

But we are at a turning point. There is growing awareness that 20th century patterns cannot be continued indefinitely. This is not least because a globalizing economy is leading to both the globalization of environmental degradation and the globalization of a constituent wishing to address it. New patterns of thought, production and consumption – some already being developed – need to be encouraged and built upon. This will require governance structures that are imaginative, responsive to change, and built on a clear vision of the links between the environment, the economy, and society. Integral to these structures must be strengthened partnerships between states, parliamentarians, civil society and business.

While present modes of economic production, trade and investment may have negative environmental and human consequences, the argument here is not that economic growth *per se* is the problem. The issue, rather, is that structures, which govern how production rate and investment occur, are inadequate to the task of protecting the environment and human life. Current economic governance structures continue to make rules that actively undermine existing environmental and social safeguards and limit the ability of national governments to respond adequately to new environmental concerns.

Considering all these emerging environmental issues

sometimes we may look back to our traditional systems where our ancestors evolved alone and survive sustainably with Nature. Thereby they lead the human civilization and its legacy. The traditional way of life always interplays with the Nature and natural environment.

Our ancestors are bound to their land by many intimate ties. Their feeling for it is something more than mere possessiveness. It is connected with their sense of history, for their legends tell of great journeys they made over the wild and lonely hills, and of the heroic pioneers who made the first clearings in the forest. The land is the mother who provides for them whatever they need in response to the labours of hands and who, when supplies run short, feeds them with a hundred and thousands of natural gifts. It is the setting of adventure in love, in hunting and in war, which can never be forgotten. Nature plays an indispensable role in the lives of the indigenous people and communities. Almost everything of daily use is derived from natural resources particularly of forest resources. In spite of increasing change, indigenous peoples' cultural practices are still deeply rooted and strongly felt as these have preserved nature and natural resources till now. Complexly adapted to these ecosystems in institutions and practices that have helped to reduce man's impact on ecology to the minimum; for millennia these cultures fostered low population growth and density, sustainable use of Bioresearches, healthy soil conditions and stable land holdings and that preserved us great diversity of these often fragile ecosystem.

Role of Traditional Systems

The traditional societies in the state of Manipur are being largely dependent upon biodiversity like land-use activities for their livelihood concerns. These traditional societies are at various stages of social evolution. Being dependent upon traditional ecological knowledge that is linked with manipulation and use of biodiversity in a variety of different ways, which forms the basis for their linkage with nature, the varied levels of refinement, depend upon the level at which the society finds itself in the social evolutionary scale. Arising from this, the traditional societies of developing world view the traditional systems as a socio-ecological system, where humans form part of ecosystem functioning.

Because of the exploitative approach from the rest of the society, economic development of traditional societies in the state has not received the kind of attention from the developmental agencies that it deserves. Currently, the economic well being of the traditional societies are increasingly threatened by 'global change' in an ecological sense and by 'globalization' of economies. This is the context in which the eco-sociological characteristics of the topographically landscaping region of Manipur need a kind of management which could link with the natural resources for sustainable development.

The concept of cultural landscape both in the hills and valley of Manipur are still a vibrant viable entity till today. The topographic landscape here has a variety of natural and human-managed ecosystems, and even 'Sacred Groves' or 'Sacred Landscapes' protected for cultural/religious reasons. It is in this context it becomes important to look at these ecosystem types, understand their functional attributes and learn lessons, which may be relevant for managing 'cultural landscapes' as an integrated socio-ecological entity, in a sustainable manner. In a state like Manipur, traditional ecological knowledge plays a pivotal role in thriving biological diversity till today. However, many of these forest-linked agro ecosystems and hydrological cycle are under intense anthropogenesis pressure. Therefore, they need to be revitalized for improving the condition. In order to ensure this, the right way for agricultural development need to be based on a value system that the society has, in socio-ecological context which they operate.

The System in Manipur

In the recent past, forest and environment of Manipur was one of the most luxuriant and resourceful in the country. This has been reflected in all the cultural and literary ethos and way of lives of every Manipuris in the state. The forest and its environmental factors of this state have continuously cherished culturally refined quality of human development in terms of art and culture, sports and martial activities and varieties of folk literature. Knowing the role of forest and environment, the then native rulers preserved and protected the natural heritages of the state with their traditional humble practices. These humble cultural practices of both the hills and plain dwellers of Manipur evolved a typical kind of system, which shows a close relationship with the Nature. The close relationship with nature, both in terms of struggle against the vagaries of nature and peaceful co-existence with nature that has led, through a very long period of evolution of indigenous culture and civilization. It is a matter of pride for us that till recently this moral order, a mutually respecting and mutually sustaining relationship with nature existed among our indigenous people in the tiny state of Manipur. Some of the remarkable preservation and conservation of eco-system practices as way of lives of the Manipuris are cited herewith for learning by the present generation with scientific and meaningful interpretations.

Indigenous people of the state of Manipur, living in some of the most remote and inaccessible villages are engaged in conserving our natural heritage and its diversity even today. As an example, almost all the hill villages where the shifting cultivation is practiced, the villagers were found to be using at least fifteen different varieties of local hill rice cultivars for thriving in their Jhumfield. These varieties of paddy were most sustainable for the prevailing local conditions, economic activities and consumption patterns. These traditional, age-old methods/techniques of cultivation and seed preservation are much more superior and sophisticated than the modern techniques and inputs. The total seeds and plants are free from diseases. Thus the villagers conserving the typical species till today. This is one of the most successful stories of local people and their heritage. Apart from the rice cultivars recorded, large varieties of medicinal herbs, edible plants are still preserved by local people traditionally for their home remedies and life aids.

Similarly, almost all the valley dwellers maintain and protect some areas as sacred groves for the village or clan's ancestral deity. This tradition has been practiced continuously since the evolution of valley settlement. Each clan or village has its own sacred groves sites and totem animals and plants are considered to be holy and hence protected religiously.

In the area of their sacred groves or culturally protected forest, no one was permitted to touch the plant or tree or being living in them. This restriction is enforced as a social taboo as well, so the protective and conservation mechanisms are quite elaborate and complex. As a result, in the recent past, almost all the forests of the Umang Lai were found to be the ideal zones for protection and conservation of our priceless biological diversed heritage. Simultaneously, a number of occupational and cultural activities, or, in short, all kinds of cultural waves and patterns, were generated as a living heritage of the indigenous valley dwellers of Manipur. All these cultural patterns and ethos clearly reflect an adaptive existence that identified humans with their natural environment as a single entity. Through these cultural motifs, indigenous people in our region practice meaningful preservation and conservation of the biological diversity, which they formed a part of.

Another important practice of the Meitei, which symbolizes and exemplifies the deep concerns for future generations is the ceremony called, Ngamu *Ushin Sinba* (the sending forth ceremony of the Meitei *Ngamu-Chana Orientallis* (Scheneilder – a small indigenous fish). In the ceremony of ancient origin, fingerling sized Ngamu with two corns of rice (one red and one white) in their mouth are released into rivers, ponds or wetlands. By this sending forth ceremony, every individual member of the family hoped that they would be protected from all unfortunate circumstances during the ensuing year. This is yet another success story in the traditional conservation of biodiversity within an indigenous knowledge system, embedded as it is within a household cultural practice. The Ngamu is a very important fish, its flesh known to have great healing and invigorating powers, in the diet of the Metei people.

Among our indigenous people, there are important ceremonies and rituals associated with the felling of trees for various purposes. Among them *Korokoshe, Chethuini* of Mao people, *Hijan Hirao* of Meitei may be mentioned. Numerous such like rituals are in existence among our people and their tradition, before cutting bamboo, plantain, etc. and even before plucking the leaves of many plants. This shows an intimate relationship with the growing trees and plants. Many plants and trees are planted within the homestead lands by cultural norms too. Thus, through these traditions many of our indigenous people are conserving each of the eco-system of their respective areas and thereby helping the conservation of eco-system of the region. Some of the typical tradition which always sustain as a living ecosystem in their respective areas are cited as below:

1. Khamkhui Land-use System

Khamkhui, a Tangkhul Village of Ukhrul District of Manipur located in a limestone belt. The village is famous for Khamkhui Cave, a limestone cavern with stalactite and stalagmite features. This village has a traditional and age-old land use code evolved by the people. The villagers always protect the top most portions of the hills and mountains as a forest canopy area while the middle of the hill slopes are used as settlement area with all domestic horticultural activities and lowermost foothill slopes are used for cultivation. This tradition is still by practice since time immemorial and since the evolution of human settlement in the area. This type of land use classification has a scientific implication. If the top of the hills and mountains are preserved as forested zone, the area will serve as a ideal watershed area. During monsoon rainwater will allow to percolate down to the layers of the soil and thereby enriching the underground water resources of the area and also maintaining the optimum water table of the area. This will influence the perennial source of water for domestic consumption as well as maintaining the soil moisture and a moderate climate in the area.

So long as the hilltops are protected or conserved with forest coverage the middle slope of the hill range were remain as the site where the community will settle durably. In the settlement area horticulture, kitchen gardening, poultry, piggery are successfully practiced. The byproduct of domestic waste, poultry and animal husbandry wastes are transformed into soil nutrients naturally to the foothill slopes where paddy cultivation is practiced. This is one of the most remarkable knowledge system of the indigenous people of Khamkhui Tangkhul to be learnt by the scientific communities.

2. Traditional Land-use System of Purul Akutpa

Purul Akutpa is a traditional village of Paomai tribe of Senapati District of Manipur settling in the upper catchment area of the Barak River. The indigenous people of Purul Akutpa practice a typical land-use system since time immemorial that they practice agri-cum-pisciculture in the lower paddy fields while the upper hill areas are kept for green coverage. The transplantation of paddy has been associated with one of the biggest annual festivals of "Paokee". On the night of Paokee unmarried youths perform friendly fights with traditional wrestling. On that particular night hour of the wrestling match, it is the desire of the unmarried females to observe silently for selecting their probable life partner. Next morning after Paokee night all the women folk work in the paddy transplantation. During the course of paddy transplantation unmarried male will join the female transplanters and negotiate for their life partnership. This kind of traditional land-use and cropping practices have been associated with their matrimonial life. This helps the village to have sustainable way of life with the surrounding natural resources.

Secondly, the Pukmai or Paomai of Purul Akutpa traditionally believed that if a family could erect big boulders in their paddy field like that of a monolithic culture the production of the field is increased.

3. Terrace Field of Mao-Songsong

Through learning by experience people of Mao-Songsong, Pudunamei and Punanamei realize the significance of Terrace type of paddy field. They commonly cultivate paddy in the terrace field while the hill slopes are used for cash crops and vegetable. While preparing the hill slope land for cultivation they always preserve the parent trees. If the oldest parent trees are enabled to be preserved in the Jhumfield, the productivity of that particular land has been increased. However, the oldest parent trees are nitrogen fixing tree commonly grown in the area. The system of terracing is as old as the evolution settlement in Songsong, Pudunamei and Punanamei. Hence, the indigenous knowledge system of the area is extremely significant for the sustainable human development of the area.

9

Keibul Lamjao National Park: A Floating Park at Peril

Introduction

Keibul Lamjao National Park (KLNP) is a very small National Park, situated along the south-eastern corner of the Loktak Lake (Ramsar site under Convention on Wetlands of International Importance 1990 and Montreaux Record), and in the core of the densely populated Valley of Manipur. The KNLP covers an area of 40 sq.km. between 24° 27' N and 24° 31' N latitude and 39° 53' and 93° 55' E longitude. It is the only natural home of the rare and endangered Brow-antler deer *(Cervus eldi eldi* (McClelland, 1842), locally known as Sangai.

Prior to 1891 Sangai was protected by a Royal decree. After 1891, when the Princely Kingdom of Manipur was under British rule the protection of Sangai was relaxed and people started hunting it. In 1934 the Manipur State Darbar banned the issue of permits for shooting Sangai as the species was on the verge of extinction. Since it is the only floating wildlife sanctuary in the world, nationally and globally draw the attention of Keibul Lamjao from the fact that it is the last resort in the wild of the *Sangai,* the Manipur brow-antlered deer which itself has the dubious distinction of being the most endangered mammal of the world. The Sangai was in fact at one stage considered to be extinct in the wild but in 1953 a small remnant herd was discovered in Keibul Lamjao by some local naturalists.

Subsequently, the Government of Manipur prohibited shooting and hunting (poaching) at Loktak Lake. This led to the creation of a sanctuary covering an area of 50 sq.km. In July 1954, the lake was reopened for shooting except the area of sanctuary (where the Sangai is found). However, after the survey of 1959 the sanctuary area was reported to be only 27/28 sq. km., in the year 1965 the area came under Protected Forest. Further, in the year 1968, additional areas of 7.68 sq. km on the north of the sanctuary were added and it makes a total area of 35.48 sq. km. In 1974, the area was declared as a Reserved Forest. Finally the Keibul Lamjao National Park was created in 1977 under the Wildlife (Protection) Act, 1972 with an area of 40 sq.km. An aerial census was conducted in the year 1975 and reported that only 14 Sangais survived. However, Sangai population has increased from 14 numbers in the year 1975 to 180 in the year 2003. Now Keibul Lamjao is the only natural home of the endangered Brow-antlered deer.

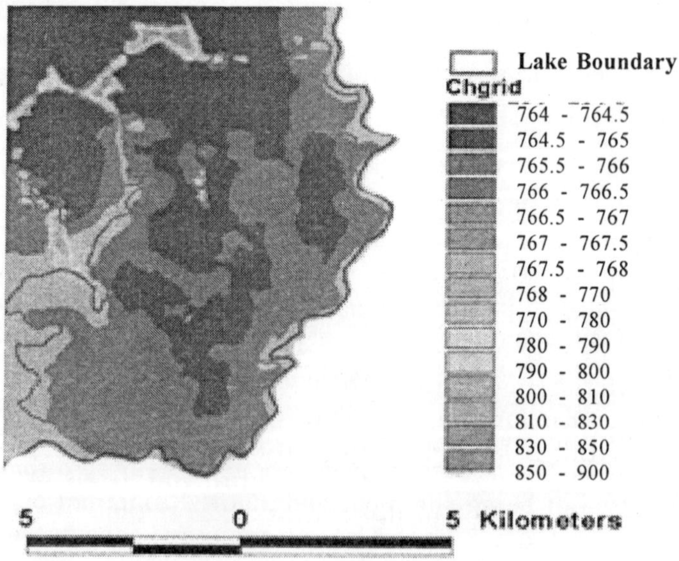

Elevation of the Keibul Lamjao Area

Brow-antlered deer of Manipur (*cervus eldi eldi)* seems to be one of the three species of Eldi deer in the world confined to South-east Asia. They are Burmese *thamin* deer (*Cervus eldi thamin*) and Siamese Brow-antlered deer (*Cervus eldi siamensis).* All the sub-species are highly engendered and believed that the three species of Brow-antlered deer originated from a single species. It is also believed that the *Cervus eldi siamensis* was first reported to be found in Thailand and migrated to Burma (Myanmar) and it is believed by the specialists that it changed some of its physical character and it is known as *Cervus eldi thamin.* Further the Burmese thamin changed its physical character when it migrated to Manipur and later known as *Cervus eldi eldi.* Thus it is the sub-species of *Cervus eldi eldi* of brow-antlered deer and has been endemic only to the Manipur valley.

Geo-ecological Setting

The Keibul Lamjao National Park is a part of the Loktak Lake. The Loktak Lake is one time, the biggest fresh water natural lake in the Eastern India. It spreads over an area of about 278 sq.km during the normal monsoon. However, during the high flood season it reaches the maximum expansion of about 490 sq.km. The probable genesis of the Loktak Lake seems to be caused by a tectonic movement resulting in the upliftment of the Manipur river bed, a few meters after the confluence of the Chakpi River near Serou. Some are of the opinion that the present valley, once part of a very much bigger lake, gradually silted up leaving the present Loktak Lake and its sister lakes in the south and southeastern portion of the Manipur Valley. Geomorphologists and geographers believe that the Loktak Lake is part and parcel of the Manipur River system. The occurrence of the Loktak and its sister lakes support varieties of biodiversities of the region. Currently, Loktak Lake itself may be treated as temporary water reservoir of the Manipur river system. It may also be compared with the lake Tonle Sap system of the Mekong River of Vietnam. The Loktak Lake is located in the interfluves area of the Khurga and the Manipur Rivers and also receives several inlets directly discharging into the Loktak. On the other hand the Khordak channel serves as **inlet and outlet** in between the Manipur River and the Loktak Lake.

The Keibul Lamjao National Park having an area of 40 sq. km lies on the southeastern side of the Loktak Lake and is located at a place of about 50 km away from the Imphal town. The villages namely Komlakhong, Arong, Tera and Khordak lie to the east of the Park; Sagram, Keibul and Chingmei villages to the west; Thanga lies to north and the Nongmaikhong, Ithai Wapokpi lie to the south. The Park consists of floating bio-mass, submerged grassland, elevated ridges and sporadic hillocks forming islets. The topographic features of the park have been characterized by floating *phumdi* (Bio-mass) covering 29 sq. km approximately, an entangled mass of reeds and weeds, three small hillocks viz. Chingjao, Pabotching and Toyaching stand inside the park and three elevated grounds

1989

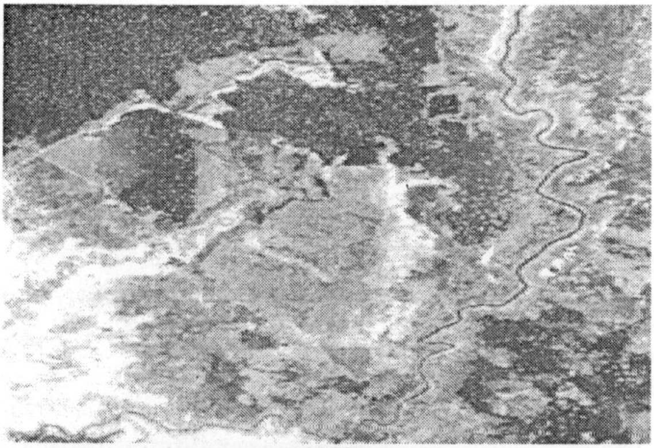

1999

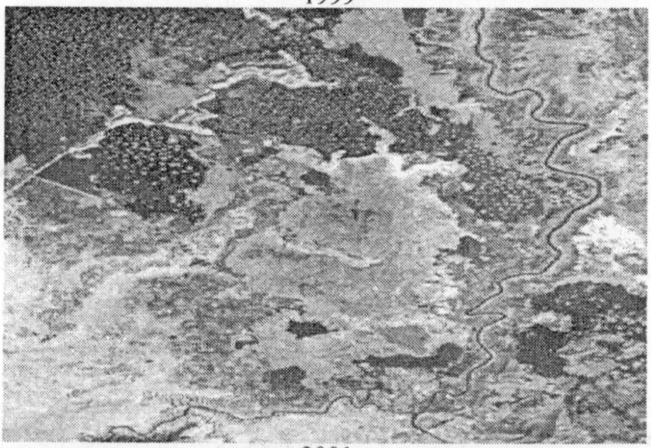

2001

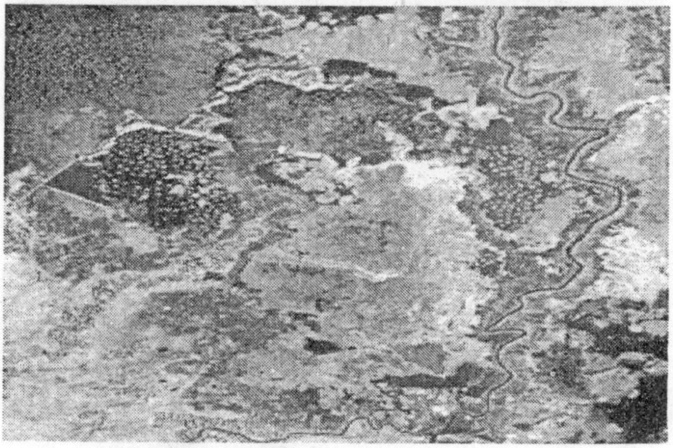

2002

Satellite Image of the Keibul Lamjao Area showing the wetlands and vegetations namely Thangbrel-Yangbi, Bogra Yangbi and Hangamhoubi Yangbi etc are located inside the park. Its altitude varies from 768m. above mean sea level at the water surface to 770m. at the ridges and to 792.5m at the top of the hills. Considering the existing landscape, the park may broadly be classified into three ecological units namely i)the ***Phumdi* unit** covering the central, western and southern areas of the park, ii) the ***Terrestrials* unit** consisting of three hillocks viz. Toyaching, Pabotching and Chingjao and iii) the ***Aquatic* unit** covering deep water area in northern sides without *phumdi*. Climatically, the park enjoy moderate cool sub-tropical monsoon climate throughout the year. Because of its uniqueness in eco-system the park is the only natural habitat of the world famous most endangered mammal, the *Brow Antlered deer* (*Cervus eldi eldi*). It is also a breeding ground of a number of riverine fish species and serves as winter home to a large avian migratory, particularly of waterfowl population in this park.

The natural hydrological cycle of the Keibul Lamjao is directly controlled by the hydrological regime of Loktak Lake. During the monsoon the water level of the Loktak rise up to a certain level and subsequently large area of phumdi (biomass) has been lifted and maintain the buoyancy. Similarly during the lean season the lake water level receded then phumdies were settling down to the lake bottom and allowing them to absorb the required nutrient. During the process a small stream call Ungamail originated from Keibul Hillock, playing an active role in draining the excess water from the Keibul Lamjao National Park.

Corresponding to the existing natural hydrological cycle, eco-landscaping, soil along with the normal climatic conditions, prevailing in the area, varieties of vegetation and its composition were made available in the Keibul

Lamjao. Floristic composition of wildlife habitat and its dynamics plays a critically significant role in the park to maintain uniqueness by providing food, shelter, breeding and playing field for the Sangai. Forest in the hillocks may be categorized as East Himalayan moist deciduous one. Vegetation coverage of phumdies is entirely different from the coverage on hillocks and lake areas. Phumdies are the floating mass of entangled vegetation, formed by the accumulation of organic debris and biomass with soil particles, which has been concentrated in a solid form. It covers approximately 2/3 to 3/4 area of the park. Its thickness varies from few centimeters to two meters. The humus of phumdi is black in colour and very spongy with large number of pores. It floats with approximately 1/5 and 4/5 part above and under water respectively. The main compositions of the phumdi are *Zizania latifolia* (Eshing kambong), *Saccharum munja* (khoimom), S. *bengalensis, Eiranthus procerus* (Singnang), *Dioschoria bulbifera* (Phumha), *Cynodon dactylon* (Tingthou), *Alpina galangal* (Pullei), *Eichornia crossipes* (Kabokang), *Hedychium coronarium* (Loklei), *Nelumbo nucifera* (Thambal), *Phragmites karka* (Tau), etc. Thus phumdi is the most important and unique part of the habitat.

Sangai and Keibul Lamjao Park

The Sangai was once found in a wide area in Manipur. In the state, Sangai has not only been persecuted by hunters but also has all along been progressively deprived of its habitat by the onslaught of reclamation of land with the continuous growth of population in the State. Granting that it is a mammal, excellently adapted in the swampy area, however, they use the terrestrials' pastures during the dry season. Sangai has been persecuted so much that it is now confined only in the Keibul Lamjao area. Even the habitation of Sangai at Keibul Lamjao confine itself is because of the safe shelters offered by the phumdies. Hence, Sangai adopted itself to making use of the phumdis for shelter particularly for breeding and also for food. In fact an ideal home range for the Sangai would be a combination of the phumdies, the hard ground pasture and the shallow lake waters. Three small hillocks viz. Chingjao and Pabot in the north and the Toya in the south of the park and three thin strips of ridges (Thangbrel yangbi, Bogra yangbi and Hangamhaubi yangbi) in the middle of the park are free from inundation. Phumdi that remain settled on the bottom of the lake throughout the dry season, do not come afloat during the early floods. They take time to soak and sober or loosen their rootlets locked with the soil in the lake-bottom. Thus for a considerable period of time during the early floods, the only resort for all the terrestrial mammals are the aforesaid three hillocks and the three thin strips of land. Further until the phumdis come afloat, the fodder is provided by these hillocks and land strips. From this point of view of both food and shelter is the pinch period for the Sangai and in fact for all the terrestrial herbivores. Obviously this combination of habitats eco-system was very much ideal in the distant past of the Manipur Valley. The endless reclamation and encroachment activities over the wetlands in combination with the degradation of catchment/watershed areas of the Loktak bound drainages and the Manipur river system; the habitat areas of Sangai have been continuously disturbed. The progressive decimation of the habitat and relentless poaching by certain groups of communities are responsible for the liquidation of Sangai.

Keibul Lamjao the natural habitat of Sangai has also been alarmingly degraded after the commissioning of the Loktak Hydro Electric Project by the NHPC. The natural eco-system of the Loktak Lake and more specifically the Keibul Lamjao National Park has been irreparably altered and damaged. The construction of the Ithai Barrage across the Manipur River, affected the normal behaviours of the river resulting shallower and shallower of the river beds of the upper stream. Subsequently, the Khordak Channel allows only inflow of debris water towards the Loktak Lake. This process has further been accelerated by the excessive deforestation in the catchment areas causing heavy siltation in to the lake. As a result more than 4.4 lakh c.u.m. of silt sediment is being brought into the Loktak every year (Loktak Development Authority LDA).

A large volume of silt particles and domestic sewage from Imphal Town is carried by the Nambul River which finally discharges into the lake. Other chemicals used in the peripheral agricultural fields are also washed off into the lake. The other factors threatening the lake are encroachments in the lake by making different fish ponds, construction of surface road across the lake and settlements which has gradually led to the shrinkage of the Loktak area. This is also one of the most menacing threats to the Loktak eco-system. On the other hand, the natural flow of the Ungamail channel has been completely altered to the opposite direction i.e. towards Keibul with huge sediment.

Since the commission of Ithai Barrage (1983) the water level of the Loktak has been constantly maintained at 769 meter. As a result the phumdies always remain floating beyond season. Because of such development projects phumdies are losing their natural cycle. Subsequently, the phumdies are becoming thinner (below the normal/desired level of thickness).

There were many reports of unnatural death of Sangai. As we know, the Sangais are natural dancer, the play ground; phumdies as such has become a threat to their life and to the extinction of the species. Because of phumdies becoming thinner accidental deaths of Sangais are reported. That, the Sangais are traped in the phumdies as the phumdies lost the natural buoyancy to support the body weight of the Sangai. As such some of the Sangais are drown to death. Therefore the ecosystem of Keibul Lamjao as a natural home for the Sangai has been drastically degraded. This may be one of the factors which may lead the National Park at peril.

Thus, observing the overall condition of the KLNP it shows that there is no appropriate policy for conservation and management of the park. At the same time taking the undue advantage of the law and order situation in the State some unlawful and illegal activists are freely accessible inside the park. To flush out such elements from the park very recently Operation Summer Storm was conducted (April 11 to 21, 2009) by the Para-military forces and reported that more than 60% of the phumdi areas were burned. This kind of activities might have caused another dimension of threat to the very existence of the Sangai are yet to be found.

Way Forward

Keibul Lamjao provides a unique eco-space for the natural habitat of the Sangai on this Earth Planet. It is also well recognized as the only floating park of the **dancing deer** in the world. Although, such a rare and endangered floating park of Sangai is located at Keibul Lamjao of Manipur, it is the heritage for all the population of the world. Hence the people of Manipur and the state government shall make an endless effort for sharing the significant task of eco-restoration and long term conservation of the Sangai and the Keibul Lamjao. However, there are many shortfalls on the part of the concerned department and also acceptability of peoples' participation on the issues of the conservation and protection of Keibul Lamjao National Park.

Considering the present scenario of the KLNP the following few approaches may be considered in the long term management perspective.

1. There should be a National Policy for conservation of Sangai and its only habitat, Keibul Lamjao.

2. Make Sangai Vision 2020 to undertake short term and immediate necessary steps for eco-restoration programme of the Sangai and its natural habitat in a scientific manner by the state government in collaboration with other institutions and agencies.

3. Lastly, the Keibul Lamjao National Park should be upgraded to the status of World Heritage Site. This is needed on account of mounting challenges for protection and conservation of the lone surviving specie of Sangai.

REFERENCES

1. H.S.Panwar, *Are Only Sangai And Keibul Lamjao Threatened? Are the People of Manipur Themselves Not?*

2. Dr.R.K. Ranjan Singh & H. Priyokumar Sharma, *Wetlands of Manipur. Vol.I.*

3. Loktak Development Authority, Manipur(LDA), *Management of Loktak Lake.*

10

Threats to Bioresources

BIORESOURCES

To understand what are Bioresources we need to understand Biological diversity or Biodiversities which refers to variety of life forms: the different plants, animals and microorganisms, the genes they contain, and the ecosystems they form. This living wealth is the product of hundreds of millions of years of evolutionary history. Biological diversity is usually considered at three different levels: genetic diversity, Species diversity and ecosystem diversity.

Genetic diversity refers to the variety of genetic information contained in all of the individual plants, animals and microorganisms. Genetic diversity occurs within and between populations of species as well as between species.

Species diversity refers to the variety of living species. At present global level scientists have identified 2.5 lakh flowering plants, 7.5 lakh species of insects, 9 thousand species of birds and 6 thousand species of reptiles.

Ecosystem diversity relates to the variety of habitats, biotic communities, and ecological processes, as well as tremendous diversity present within ecosystem in terms of habitat differences and the variety of ecological processes. Ecosystem diversity depends on geographic location, climatic conditions. There are different types of Ecosystems. Each Ecosystem has itsown distinct inter-linked species and each ecosystem varies structurally and functionally.

Biodiversity- the variety of life and of habitats on Earth- is vital to human welfare. Biodiversity loss also has social consequences, in its impact on people's livelihoods and life styles – this is the unmeasured cost of losing cultural traditions. The loss of key elements of an ecosystem can alter the balance between its components and lead to long-term or permanent changes. Biodiversity loss can also affect human health, as our health is largely dependent on the quality of ecosystem in which we live. Loss of plant or animal species can affect the quality of water or soil.

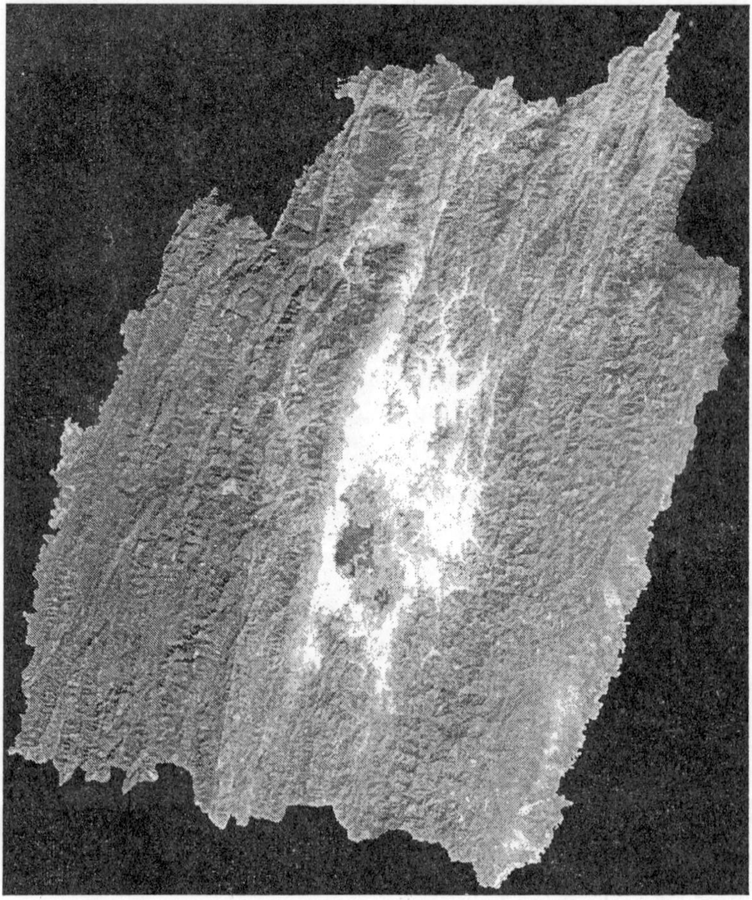

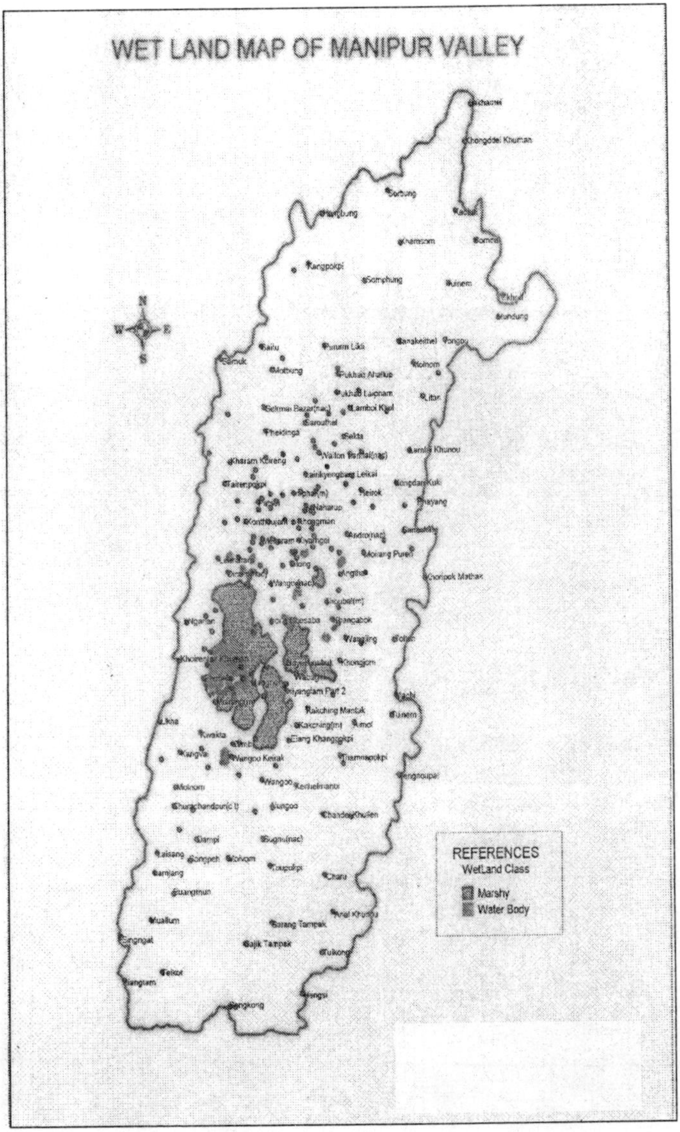
WET LAND MAP OF MANIPUR VALLEY
REFERENCES
WetLand Class
Marshy
Water Body

Indo-Burmese (Myanmar) Hotspot

Sl.No.	Particulars	
1	Original extent of Primary Vegetation	2,000,000 km2
2	Remaining Primary Vegetation & p.c. of Original extent	100,000 km2 (4.9%)
3	Area protected & p.c. of Hotspot	100,000 km2 (100%)
4	Plant species	13,500
5	Endemic plants & p.c. of global plants	7,000 (2.3%)
6	Vertebrate species	2,185
7	Endemic vertebrates & p.c. of global vertebrates	528 (1.9%)

Area – 22,327 km2
(91.75% hills; 8.25% valley)
Rainfall – 131 cm/year
Altitude – 800 to 3,300 metres above MSL

- **4000 Angiospermic plants**
- **430 Medicinal plants**
- **500 Orchids**
- **55 Bamboo species**
- **40 Endemic rice cultivars**
- **160 fish species**
- **21 Wild birds**
- **20 Medicinal zingiberales**
- **Multitudes of low/high altitude butterflies**

Burned Hill slope for Jhuming

Trapping and Killing of Moorfalconat and migratory birds

Trapping and Killing of Moorfalconat and migratory birds

Yangkhullen Chief's House decorated with Trophies

Moorhen, Phubala

Dzuko Valley

Today, as ever, human beings are dependent for their sustenance, health, well-being and enjoyment of life on fundasmental biological systems and processes. These fundamental biological systems and processes may broadly be termed as Bioresources. In another words humanity derives all of its food and many medicines and industrial products from the wild and domesticated components of biological diversity. Therefore, Bioresources attributes means of attaining satisfaction of individual wants or social objectives, resource relates to man and its functional and the end result must be beneficial. For example, Water, is a resource not because of its color, composition but because of its function of satisfying some of human wants.

Threats

The main threats on biodiversity result from land use changes (usually associated with increasing population); unsustainable use and exploitation of natural resources (especially fisheries, agriculture, and forestry); global climate change; and industrial pollution. At the same time, biotechnology is introducing new organisms and their effect on existing organisms and habitats also needs to be considered as a threat. The available evidence suggests that, in most regions of the world, the effects of economic activities are negative on biodiversity and degrading the Bioresources. The policy brief looks at what governments can do to place a value on and help preserve biodiversity and ensure sustainable Bioresources.

Biodiversity and Bioresources in general are more dispersed and less easily targeted for collective policy. There is also less room for error- if air becomes more polluted, steps can be taken to reduce the pollution, but if an ecosystem is compromised by human activities; its loss may be permanent. Given that our knowledge of the complexity and inter-linkages of ecosystems are only cursory, loss of biodiversity and bioresources may be more important than any *short term political economy* gains. Before policy makers take decisions about whether to risk destroying a habitat for short term gain of political economy (such as construction of Dams across the river for hydroelectric power generation and any kind of development etc) they need to be able to set a relative value for those gains and for the biodiversity at risk.

In Manipur

Geographically, Manipur is a unique land of Mountains with intermittent river valleys and plains. This area has been evolved with a typical natural environmental factor. Through this environmental framework, the area creates specific geo-climatic regions of endemic flora and fauna and an ideal home for the indigenous settlers. The hilly or mountain region occupies 80% of the state's total area of 22,327 Sq.Km. with average elevation ranging from 1000 m.a.m.s.l. to 3000 m.a.m.s.l. The mount Esso is the highest peak (3002m) while Dzuku valley the highest dale (2500m) of the state. The whole area of the state has been classified and codified into 35 different watershed areas as per national norms. These watershed areas are along the two major drainage systems of the state i.e. the Barak and the Manipur River. Each and every codified watershed areas of the state has its own endemic species with typical habitat. Till today we are not able to document its flora and fauna and its microbes scientifically. However, some of the scientific studies of the State of Manipur were recorded since 1889. Ward F. Kingdon reported 143 plant species, Clarke reported 1050 flowering plants and 114 ferns, Deb added another 1500 plant species (1957-1961), Baishya and Sukla added 43 new species of flowering plants and 13 cryptograms (1984), A.C. Sinha added 523 plant species further (1987), Bikram added 667 new plant species (1988-89),Kumar reported 31 wild edible plant species (2001). Similarly faunal species are also adding more. But unfortunately the current trend of loss and extinction of flora and fauna are also increasing day by day.

11

Tipaimukh High Dam Across the Barak River

Introduction

The Tipaimukh High dam (THD) is proposed to be constructed across the Barak river 500 m downstream from the confluence of its tributary the Tuivai river in the southwestern corner of Manipur State (24°14'N and 93°01.3'E) bordering Mizoram and Assam states. The Barak is a trans-boundary river having a total length of about 900 km. Of this 525 km falls within North East India. The Barak system is the second largest drainage system in NE having a drainage basin area of about 52000 sq. km. in India and 12000 sq. km. in Bangladesh (64,000 sq. km.).

The main headstream originated from Lai-Liyai village of Senapati District of Manipur and upper stream catchment areas of the Barak spreading all over the western half of the Manipur State covering all the inhabited areas of indigenous people of Senapati, Tamenglong, Churachandpur districts and Jiribam Sub-division of the State.

The flood-plain and middle course of the Barak were located with Cachar, Karimganj and Hailakandi districts of Lower Assam. Its important right-bank tributaries include Makru, Jiri, Labak, Madhura, Dalu, Jatinga and Larang etc. The major left-bank tributaries are Irang, Tuivai, Sonai, Rukni, Katakhal, Dhaleswari, Singla, and Langai.

The lower course of the Barak started when it enters Bangladesh near Amalshid of Sylhet district and bifurcates into two streams namely the Surma River and the Kushiara river. The Surma and the Kushiara rivers reunite near Markuil in Habiganj district and becomes the Kalni River. The entire riverine-ecosystem of the *Barak River Basin* supports an endemic agrarian civilization thriving on biodiversity-based agro-ecological systems that have profound local and global significance.

Main Feature of THD

The THD project envisions a 390 m long, 162.8 m high earthen-rock filled dam across the Barak. The dam will be at an altitude of about 180 m above mean sea level with a maximum reservoir level of 178 m. The dam was originally designed to contain floodwaters in the lower Barak Valley but hydro power generation was later incorporated into the project. The project will have an installation capacity of 6X250=1500 MW and a firm generation of 412 MW. The dam will permanently submerge an area of 275.50 sq. km. in the state of Manipur.

Axis Site

There is no Proper or Complete study that focuses on the geo-tectonic, biodiversity and environment, health, socioeconomic and hydrological impact of the entire Barak Basin. The absence of meaningful consultation with the indigenous people contradicts the first strategic priorities developed by the WCD on Dam *no dam should be built without the demonstrable acceptance of the affected people, and without the free PRIOR AND INFORMED CONSENT.*

Groups in Manipur from all communities have resisted Tipaimukh High Dam for more than 15 years. The arguments are as follows:

Map Source: Down to Earth

THD Dam

1. The struggle against THD is not a new phenomenon but began in early 1990s, nor is it an imitation of anti-dam struggles in other parts of the world. When it began, it was because the people of Manipur have seen the devastating impact of ***Loktak Hydro Electric Project***. This project has been one of the single most factors that make people to begin questioning the new project THD. Any person who is aware of ***Loktak Hydro Electric project*** will tell you how it has submerged large tracts of agricultural lands not only ousting large number of farmers from their livelihood without compensation but also reducing self-sufficiency in rice production, apart from devastating a fragile wetland ecosystem. This has further made Manipur more economically dependent on mainland India, which is just the opposite of the promise made when the project was conceived. The people of Manipur are now fully aware that Manipur gets so little electricity not even to light up every home. In addition, we are now waking up to the fact that ***Mapithel Dam*** (***Thoubal Multipurpose Project***) and ***Khuga Dam*** also have not only deceived the people but that even after 20 years of 'construction' these have not yielded any result. Now we see how wrong decisions made in the past can create havoc for our future. By now, the struggle against THD is not restricted to Manipur only but also in Mizoram and Bangladesh too, where the immediate impact of the Dam will be felt.

2. This dam was in the first place not a dam conceived and designed for the people of Manipur or for that matter for Mizoram or for the people of NE. It was initially designed to control flood in lower Assam, and then to generate electricity for the Indian state owned NEEPCO for sale outside the region. For all these years the dam builders have not informed and consulted the people of Manipur and Mizoram especially those

who are going to be impacted directly. The dam is imposed. It is not based on internal or local requirements but an insert from above that will serve economic interest that none knows. An issue of consent is a must when they want to bring in a project of such magnitude that will submerge villages, fertile agricultural land, forest etc. Local people and organizations have also proposed alternative of other dams of smaller nature that will be less destructive.

3. If one closely looks at the resettlement and rehabilitation plan of NEEPCO, it is clear that they have not taken into account intergenerational concerns. For example, rice fields cannot be compensated at today's market price only, as it is done by NEEPCO. For we all know that a plot of land has benefited both the generation in the past and will serve our future and cannot be assessed for the present market value only. A mere lakh or two will only create impoverishment and hardship for those displaced. A more important issue is close link of Indigenous People to their land, water, forest and their culture. Any sizeable loss of land is loss of the community itself.

4. If the Government of Manipur is keen on developing a sound project(s) for development and here in this case for electricity, then it must have widespread consultation to decide on the electricity requirement for now and for future, and then decide on the presently available technological options such as hydro, wind, solar etc to obtain that requirement. THD does not fit into this people friendly energy decisions. We must insist that THD is not an answer to the energy crisis that we presently face and that if the Government is sincere enough to solve this crisis then it must right away say no to THD and initiate a people inclusive dialogue on energy.

5. Dams as known elsewhere have created or accentuated ethnic conflict. True to this nature of dams, here too, there are already divisions along ethnic lines that can have long-term implications for all people. In an already fractured place it is imperative that the state takes a more positive action that does not allow projects that widened ethnic divide. In addition, conflict with Mizoram, Assam and also with Bangladesh as a result of the dam cannot be ruled out and will need to be addressed before agreeing to the project.

6. The dam, if constructed, will have negative impact on an area of 9,126 square km. in the state of Manipur alone. A large number of indigenous communities, mostly belonging to the Zeliangrong and Hmar people, will be permanently displaced and deprived of their livelihood. One should be aware that these affected areas are almost half of the present size of Manipur. A small state like Manipur cannot afford to bargain this area for a tiny bit of electricity. We must look for alternative source of energy where it has least impact on land. Remember we already have 60,000 Hectares of agricultural land submerged due to **Ithai Barrage** only. For our food security we cannot afford to lose anymore land.

7. We are also aware that dams' construction brings in laborers from outside the region. We are witness to that the fact that outsiders have come to work for ***Loktak Hydro Project***, Mapithel, Khuga etc and that these workers have stayed back and have created demographic concerns. A massive project like THD will bring in more than 30,000 workers from outside and it is certain that these outsiders will stay on and settle.

8. The site selected for THD project is one of the most active seismic zone in the entire world, recording at least two major earthquakes of 8+ in the Richter scale

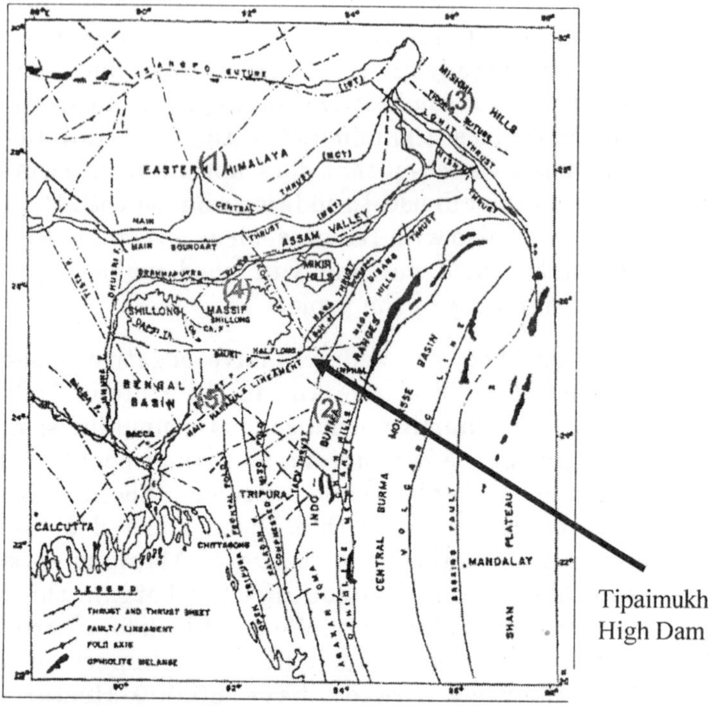

Tectonic Setting of North-east India

(1) Eastern Himalayan Collision Zone

(2) Indo-Myanmar Subduction Zone

(3) Syntaxis Zone

(4) Shillong Plateau, Mikir Hills and Assam Valley Zone

(5) Bengal basin and Tripura-Mizoran Fold Belt

during the past 50 years. The proposed THD is envisaged for construction in one of the most geologically unstable area as the proposed THD axis falls on a 'fault line' potentially active and possible epicenter for major earthquakes. Several earthquakes over magnitude 5-7 were recorded within a radius of 6 km to 100 km of Tipaimukh in the past 150 years and the epicenter of the last earthquake in 1957, with a magnitude of 8 lies at approximately 80 km from the dam site in an east-northeast direction. Since the dam site is located at the Manipur-Mizoram-Assam bordering with Burma, it is apprehended that the project would make impact on watershed area of Burma as well, thus influencing the ecological aspect of Burma's northern area. The historic Old Cachar Road, popularly known as Tongjei Maril and traditional waterways along the Barak will be disconnected from the state capital and the upper Barak forever.

The people who have fought the dam have used all democratic means possible to seek the Government of India to stop the dam. Memoranda and letters in scores, rallies, sit-in protest, blockade, strike, press releases, meetings, leaflets, e-mail campaign etc. have been used. Five Public hearings conducted by the government have been boycotted. But these all went into the dustbin of the government. One wonders whether there is any other form and ways where one can stop the dam.

12

Endangered Languages of Manipur

The northeast India is located in a crossroad where chains of human migration had been taken place from different directions during the distant past. If one probes the process of peopling of the region one can discern eleven major streams and waves of immigration which had built up the present ethnic communities in the north-east India. As a result ethnolinguistically diverse groups descending from the people who have immigrated from different directions since early time inhabited in the region. It is believed that the first ever group of people settled in this region in the pre-historic past is the *Mon Khmer,* whose descendents are today identified as *Khasis.* They were followed by the *Tibeto-Burman* language-speaking people of the *Sino-Tibetan,* who immigrated from the north and the east. Most of the tribes of the hills and plains of the region belong to this group. Thirdly, came the *Indo-Aryans,* who started settling in this region. Then the waves of migration were followed by different groups like *Tai-Ahom, Sino-Siamese* etc. Hence, the present population of the region is essentially made of the above eleven streams and waves of migration resulting in a mosaic of sociocultural patterns. The emerging sociocultural scene is such that the population of the region can be divided into 357 constitutional communities including 32 scheduled castes and 182 scheduled tribes.

Similarly the state of Manipur has also been located in

the east-west immigrant corridors, different ethno-linguist communities were inhabited since pre-historic time. Manipur traditionally is the home of *Meiteis'* and other 33 officially recognized tribes and sub-tribes. All these communities are having their own mother tongues while *Meiteilon* (Manipuri the state Language) is used as *lingua-franca* for all the communities who settled in the state. All these different mother tongues belong to Tibeto-Burman (TB) sub-family of the Sino-Tibetan family. There are more than 100 communities speaking different TB languages in the northeastern States mainly in Arunachal Pradesh, Mizoram, Nagaland and Manipur. Around 20 TB languages are having the population less than 5000 speakers; it means they are becoming endangered languages. Some of the languages or dialects are not yet fully described and some are near to extinct.

Generally, the fundamental cause for the disappearance of a language or dialects is well known. The community themselves abandon their native tongue in adaption to an environment where use of that language is no longer advantageous to them. Secondly, at the national level there is urgent need of framing a language policy which could cater the need of preserving and revitalization of the endangered languages of the nation. Globalization and its impact on the culture further accelerate the extinction of minority languages. In Manipur, there are many endangered languages. According to 2001 census the following tribes' mother tongues are in the stage of being endangered.

1. Aimol: Inhabited in 3 districts of the state with a population of about 2,643 (2001): Chandel, Senapati and Churachandpur. Aimol Khullen, Unapal, Satu, Kumirei, Chingunghut, Aimol Tampak, Khodampai, Ngairong, Chandonpokpi, Soibong in Chandel district and Tuikhong in Senapati district. Kai-Aimol and Luichungbum in Churachandpur.

2. Chothe: Inhabited in 15 villages of Chandel district with a population of about 3,600 (2001). They are Khongkhang, Chandonpokpi, Lunghu, Lirungtabi, Zunthang, Ajouhu, Punthapokpi, Laininghu, Chandrapoto, Tampokhu, Lamlangghupi, Old Wangparal, New Wangparal, Lungle and one village in Bishnupur district.

3. Koireng: Inhabited in Saikhul, Kangpokpi and Longa Koireng in Senapati district, Moirang in Bishnupur district and Pallel in Chandel district with a population of about 1,056 (2001).

4. Kom: Inhabited in east and central Manipur, Churachandpur, Tamenglong and Senapati districts with a population below 4000 (2001).

5. Monsang: Inhabited in Liwachaning, Heibunglok, Liwa Sarei, Lapho, Monsang Pantha of Chandel district with a population of about 3,200 (2001).

6. Moyon: Inhabited in 14 villages of Chandel district. They are namely Moyon Khullen, Khongjom, Mitong, Heigru Tampak etc with a population of about 3,700 (2001).

7. Purum: Inhabited in Purum Chumpang, Purum Khullen, Purum Tampak, and Purum Changningtoy of Chandel district with a population of about 503.

8. Simte: Inhabited in Mingjang, Tabuong, Simveng, New Banazar, Thanglon, Leikangpai, Zouthang, Shumtuk, Monjon and Panjal of Churachandpur district.

9. Tarao: Inhabited mainly in Chandel district. Villages are Tarao khullen (Tarao Laimanai, Leishokching, Khuringmol and Heikamul with a population of about 870 (2001).

10. Kharam: Inhabited in Kharam Pallen, East Laikot

(Chabungkhong) of Tamenglong district and Seijang of Ukhrul and Imphal districts of Manipur.

Languages of a community are closely associated with its Prevailing Cultural practices in the community itself. Diversity of languages and dialects are the heritage wealth of a nation. So the diversities should be maintained since India is a land of diversities in languages, culture and traditions. The endangered languages should be made documentation. Once a community lost its surrounding, its knowledge of the environment (say, herbal medicine, folk medicine and other indigenous knowledge system) is lost. Hence, it is high time for us to take care of and to make documentation of all the endangered languages and traditions for the future generation.

13

Natural Resources Based Development Strategies: Problems and Prospects of Manipur

Current Scenario of Developmental Process

Lopsided developmental processes in the State of Manipur have led to vast inequalities, leaving almost 80 per cent of the geographical area in under-developed zone. This underdeveloped geographical area belongs to the hilly terrain topographic region, predominantly settled by the indigenous highland communities. Ninety per cent of the total population of the highland communities is underprivileged and victims of poverty. They remain underdeveloped in the midst of bountiful natural resources surrounding their habitat areas. Similarly 80 per cent of the rural population of the valley-dwelling communities are neither able to enjoy the fruits of development programmes nor able to take active role in the development processes of the state. From time to time different phases of development efforts were made to improve the State as a whole, or sectors through people's participation.

Firstly, attempts were made to develop hill and backward areas and measures were initiated to develop these areas. Secondly, there were efforts to create democratic institutions to decentralize the power and ensure people's participation in the development programmes. Thirdly, there were attempts for creating growth centers. Fourthly, there were schemes in the form of special projects or special rural development programmes. Fifthly, voluntary organizations, self-help groups and NGOs were encouraged to undertake development programmes. Finally, at present the efforts are on to privatize the public organizations' services and withdrawal of the state's role from its socioeconomic responsibilities. The underlying ideas of all these phases of development approaches, except the last are have been to use public for creating a self-sustainable society. However, the New Economic Policy of 1991 has changed the direction and process of people's participation in the development. More emphasis was given to privatization and liberalization etc. and use of information technology (knowledge-based economy) for development. The issues related to the need of structural changes in our society along with governance reforms being envisaged today. Even then participation in the development process widens the gap between developed and underdeveloped areas like Hill and Valley; urban and rural as they dictate the nature, location and utilization of the projects.

The method and institutions of developmental technologies of the State had become independent; however the overall continual growth of the State is mainly receiving negative impact. When thirst could no longer be quenched by water but only by mineral water, when the demand for education was perceived as a demand for schooling, and when people's own capabilities of healing, travelling, building houses and burying their dead – present in all societies in history – were lost because they were monopolized by guilds of experts, then a radical monopoly was in place. As a result, industrial production kept people dependent on industrial products and led to ever more helpless situation among them. Every coin spent on the school system means more privileges for the few at the cost of many, because these schools were available to only a small section of the population.

A transport system aimed at ever-faster individual traffic produced traffic jams, accidents, deaths, dying forests and hindered the movement of cyclists and pedestrians. Similarly, once traffic/motorable road introduced in the far-flung remotest villages, and then the village has been continuously invaded by surplus products from developed areas in a disguised form of supply. Ultimately, the primary production system of the area/village has been crumbling down and turning the people into passive consumer with an accelerated rate of consumption. After the collapse of the primary product of the area the monopolized productions make the people more dependent.

Similarly, the allopathic system monopolized the healthcare system so that even simple healing methods were reserved for specialist class. Ironically, a growing number of ailments were caused by so-called professional medical treatment. Thus, the developing society created prosperity, but impoverished the one whose resources were too scarce to be shared by all and destroyed their freedom and rights. The impact of developmental planning simply had to be convivial. It has to be acceptable without any expert's license or compulsion or violation of other people's right to freedom. Till today, the development processes and institutions remain rooted in orthodox perceptions. The finding for development and implementing agencies both hope for more from the same thing. Under free and compulsory education of constitutional provision, it is usually perceived as more finding and crating many avenues for expenditure in the name of total literacy programme etc. Similarly under better health care system, more doctors and more infrastructural developmental expenditure has been incurred. But most of the people were suffering without any treatment and compelled to go outside the State for treatment. Therefore, the goals of development policy are always far from target, in every corner of the State, measured according to the consumer value and the service facilities extended. As a result, privileged sections of the people were vividly reflected out from the total populace. In a sense development policies serve as a tool for modernizing poverty with higher degree of dependency and consumerism thereby creating more and more expansion of underdeveloped areas. This process of underdevelopment creates the basic essential needs out of the reach of the common people negating the fundamental right of a citizen. Under such circumstances, some of the politicalized planners are trying to impose certain kind of project at the cost of people's right to environment and the fundamental right of a citizen. It is in contravention to universal concept of development. The providers of infrastructural facilities should have the idea of catalyzing the capacities of the people to generate income and scope for self-sustainable development rather than to suppress the activities for participation on the process of self-sustainable development. Currently, what we have observed is that other outside productions to the area in the form of raw material from forest and dumping of other outside productions to the area in the form of 'essential commodities' etc. As for example, the Border Road passing through Kharasom (Ukhrul) connecting Kohima via Phek Chakachang area to Ukhrul influences the educated youth to extract the rich pine forest of Kharasom and export the forest resources to the business and trader groups for some tidy amount with the aims for procuring motorbike. After buying the motorbike, to meet the fuel cost the youths always demand even the hard earn money of their parents. Finally, their primary forests were degraded, their natural fresh air has been polluted with carbon monoxide, whereas, the hard earned incomes of their parents were exhausted and ultimately their livelihoods were put under extreme conditions. Hence, this kind of developmental effect will always deviate from the common goal of sustainable development of the Nation. Similarly, in the rural valley and foothill areas of the State, once a motorable road is extended, some of the prominent peasants of the area have sold out their paddy fields, and shifted to towns. At the beginning a little domestic surplus production of the area was marketed to the urban areas. But simultaneously large-scale production materials from the urban CBD area were flowing into the villages. In the later stage, there were endless free flows of materials from the urban CBD area and flooding the rural area. Ultimately, the primary products of the rural area were turned into sick sector. Traditionally the State was sufficient for good and safe drinking water. However, after the strengthening of the Department of Public Health Engineering, Government monopolized the supply of drinking water. But till today none of the water supply schemes were successfully operating in the practical sense. A large number of women folk in both urban and semi-Urban areas are seen waiting in long queues daily for getting a few litres of water from the public hydrant points. Most of the man-days were spent in waiting the 'Pipe Water'. Surprisingly, most of the local ponds, tanks, which were once conserved by both the individual household and the community were not used and filled with earth and reclaimed for other purposes. Consequently, neither the State Water Supply Schemes nor the local traditional system could provide safe drinking water with which the state could have prevented all the water borne diseases occurring in the State.

The present day patterns of governance in the state may also make manifold handicaps in the functioning of the sustainable development processes. Some groups of thinkers say that developmental planning in the state is simply projecting the budget but not the physical growth or achievement. A huge expenditure was continuously incurred for construction of road and other different projects. However, all these projects are in blue prints only. It is also a fact that most of the developmental funds were utilized for service and salaried sector but not for accelerating the overall growth sector of the State. Another group says that most of the institutions do not like to submit or prepare developmental projects because of the law and order and insecure situation prevailing in the State currently. Taking for example, all the approved development projects were continuously threatened by some elements either to get contract work or to get monetary percentages from all kinds of projects. To negotiate and convince the element is nothing but simply risking the life of the personnel. Some opine that the process of developmental planning in the State is just simply adopted without analyzing the suitability, mindset and culture of the people of the area. Most of developmental planning in almost all the plan period was not aware by the people of the State. There is no feedback or monitoring mechanism to assess the entire development project in the State. As a result, people's participation on the state development process is negligible. There is a good feeling that government belongs to the bureaucratic officials and politicians but not to the people. In a democratic country, the government without people's participation is simply meaningless.

Selection and implementation of specific area development projects or location of growth centers in the State seems to be biased and located mostly in the controversial areas. Selections for establishment of an institution are always politicalized and are carried out under pressure politics. Selection of industrial growth centres in the midst of a vast paddy field, locations of Central Agricultural University's Head Office etc. are the best examples of biased selection of specific development projects. This kind of selection neither catalyzes nor support to the process of expansion of physical growth of the State. Rather it will create higher degree of congestion to the already congested Imphal area at the same time abusing the extremely limited productive arable land mostly, say the paddy fields of the Napet-Palli of the Imphal East. Further a huge amount has been spent on payment of compensation for acquisition of privately owned land. Thus, in the process both the development growth and objective of the planning have been put into the journey to the lake of no return.

Considering all the above-mentioned aspects, the nature of development processes and its effects in the State need a new task of development strategies. New development strategies should be an alternative way of satisfying needs and sustainable growth of the State and the people as well. It is also true that, humanity possesses the knowledge and the skill to relieve the suffering of poverty of the common people. The underprivileged groups of the people have a right to expect solution to their poverty. The new development strategies may also be initiated by learning from the past efforts and question of development planning relevance. While making alternative planning policies like poverty eradication strategies, special attention should be paid to education and health of the people.

A New Attempt in Development Strategies in the State

An alternative planning shall have to be evolved, and it has to be based on the finding of the assessment of availability of natural resources of the State along with the mindset of the people and their full participation. In short, this kind of planning strategy may be termed as natural resources based development strategies. Such development strategies shall have the following purposes to achieve the desired goal of the development.

1. One of the most fundamental purposes of this planning strategy is to create will and determination of collective participation of community to improve their present and future life.
2. To identity and develop local resources to generate self-reliance among the members of the community.
3. To mobilize available human resources for productive and meaningful activities.

4. To encourage people to develop their own confidence and become self-reliant which is key to sustainable development.
5. To make the people most powerful in managing their environment and natural resources, ensure socioeconomic justice to all the members of the community.

The goals of the natural resources based development strategies include freedom from economic dependency and any other economically exploitative mechanisms; humanizing the society; promotion of self-respect; guarantee of human freedom; resolving contradictions in the society; bring about changes in the institutional, social, economic and administrative structures etc. The realization of these goals depends not only on evolving a suitable strategy covering all aspects of people and their resources, but also on the active participation of the people in the decision-making and implementation of the development programmes.

Assessing the Natural Resources

In this article, an attempt is being made to address a proper development through the availability of natural resources and its potentialities. It will also analyze the indigenous knowledge system applied by the people on the use of their natural resources. However, the application of indigenous knowledge must go hand in glove with modern science and technological inputs, so that the proposed new development strategies could transform the State in a meaningfully sustainable one.

At present Manipur is one of the North Eastern States of India. It was a princely independent State till the Anglo-Manipur War of 1891. After the war of 1891 Manipur was under the British rule up to 1947. Then a Native State was formed during 1947 to 1948 till it was merged to the Indian Union on 15th October 1949. During 1949 to 1966

Manipur was a Part-C – centrally administered and 1966 to 1972 was a Union Territory of India. Only after 1972, Manipur could be able to exercise for developmental planning as a full-fledged State of India. Only from the period of the 5th Five-Year Plan. Planning was able to join directly by the State while the rest of the Indian States achieved FIRST to FOURTH i.e. 20 years' of development was already advanced. As a result, it seems that during the initial phases of five-year planning processes in the State are of allochthonous in nature. There was no meaningful participation of the people.

The State is located in a tri-junction zone of mainland India sub-continent, Himalayan and Trans-Himalayan and Indo-Malayan genesis. A wide range of natural heritages of rare and endemic species of flora and fauna is visible in the State. The richness in natural resources is the product of its geographical location and peculiar topographic exposition of drainage patterns and wetland system of the State. Topographically the State may be grouped into two physiographic units, namely the valley of Manipur and the surrounding mountain ranges. The valley is approximately 2,640 sq. km and dotted with a number of wetlands and glittering lakes including the biggest freshwater lake of eastern India i.e. the Loktak Lake (one of the Ramsar Sites). The valley of Manipur represents hardly 20 per cent of the State's total geographical area of 22,327 sq. km. The 1000 metres contour is taken as the outer limit of the valley of Manipur. More than 75 per cent of the total human population of the State is concentrated in the valley.

(A) Resources of Hilly Region

The hilly or mountainous region occupies a large portion of the State with an area of 19,687 sq. km. This is about 80 per cent of the State's total geographical area with elevation ranging from 1000 m above m.s.l. to 3000 m above m.s.l. The Mt. Essii is the highest peak (3002 m) while Dzuku valley the highest dale (2500 m) of the State. Less than 30 per cent of the total population of the State is scattered all throughout the 80 per cent of the State's total area.

The State is located in the catchment areas of the two major drainage systems namely the Ganga-Brahmaputra and the Chindwin-Irrawady. The western half of the State falls in the catchment area of the Barak River system of the former drainage syste. The eastern half including the valley of Manipur lies in the catchment area of the Manipur River system of the Chindwin-Irrawady drainage system. In all the interfluves region of the Manipur River system of the valley region there are a number of wetlands. The existence of a number of wetlands in the valley of Manipur itself is a unique natural feature of the State.

The vast track of the Manipur Hills and the wetlands of the Manipur Valley are yet to be considered as one of the richest potential natural resources for sustainable development in the State. Rather this vast hilly terrain tracks and wetland areas of the State are normally treated as wasteland from the present day context of developmental planning process.

Mountain terrains of Manipur might seem like impenetrable monoliths of rock but in reality, they are among the nation's greatest sources of biodiversity, having varieties of plants, animals and microorganisms. Many of these species have disappeared from the valley area due to increase in population and increased human activities. The primary guardians of these irreplaceable biodiversities are the highlanders of Manipur. Until now, our developmental planners and the government have generally overlooked the knowledge that our highlanders possess of the important role that hilly terrain play in preserving most of the natural resources of the State.

Isolation and relative inaccessibility have helped to protect and preserved bio-resources in the hilly terrains of the Manipur State. Large varieties of native hill rice cultivars are still thriving in the hills and are the best species for security of the hill dwellers. Many wild edible vegetables, herbs and ferns are abundantly growing in the area. A number of medicinal plants and herbs are grown and used by the indigenous highland people effectively for their live saving. Varied species of Orchids, which are of endemic nature, are growing in the hills of Manipur. For the last many centuries the highlanders are conserving and using them with the application of their indigenous knowledge system. These precious genetic reserves are our insurance for the future, particularly as the present trend of development turns into the habit of consumerism and dependency. Here the author of this paper may be permitted to quote as follows:

> "A farmer lived in the mountains, another on the plain. The plainsman, in the forefront of all that was modern, swapped all his seeds for ones they said were better. The mountain man kept planting his same old seeds.
>
> How Backward can you get?
>
> And then one day, the crops in the plain just died. And so, to the mountain man, the valley dweller went for begging. For treasures lay hidden in that rustic's seeds: treasures to give everyone a better life (A modern fable)".

There are documented records where varied medicinal plants like *Panax pseudo-ginseng, Coptis teeta* Wall, *Taxus baccata* Linn, *Kaempferia rotunda L., Gonithalamus seswuipedalis* Hook. F., etc. were abundantly available in the hills of Manipur. These species are of high value in the world market. From these natural resources people of the highland may generate their income if the planner thought it seriously with the feasible science and technology intervention. It is also recorded that throughout the hilly terrains of Manipur there are more than 55 bamboo species. These bamboo species are of high potential for extracting steroidal drugs. Utilizing the bamboo as a natural resource, the state and the people could capture the world market from bamboo-based foods, drug formulation or bamboo based art and craft of indigenous character. Similarly, crises of energy may be solved to a great extent by utilizing the cheaply available bamboo. At the same time attention should be given to protecting the intellectual property rights of the communities, whose indigenous knowledge has been the source of profit for others who introduced these products into the world market.

Scientific floristic studies of the State of Manipur were recorded since 1889. Ward reported 143 plant species, Clarke reported 1050 flowering plants and 114 ferns, Deb (1957-1961) reported 1500 plant species, Baishya and Sukia (1984) added 523 new plant species, Bikram added 667 plant species, while Kumar (2001) reported 31 wild edible plant species. Now altogether Manipur State have been recorded with 4000 angiospermic plants, 430 medicinal plants, 500 orchids, 55 bamboo species, 40 endemic rice cultivars, 160 fish species, 20 medicinal zingiberales. Based on this information the application of Science and Technology like Germplasm/Tissue culture technique may be extended from the laboratory to field effectively.

Over the generations people of Manipur have accumulated a wide range of knowledge about sustainable development based on their surrounding environment and natural resources. Practices such as shifting cultivation in the hills sustained the people of highland for centuries. However, *Jhumming* (shifting cultivation) practices need modernization to catch the changing circumstances and appropriate land-use practices. Traditional land-use practices always incorporated an understanding of local conditions and their immediate surroundings. However, age-old Jhum practices in the hills of Manipur could not maintain their own customary code of land-use/Land Laws for quite a long time. As a result, at present, the customary land laws were extremely put to stretches and strains by the imposition and implementation of the so-called development processes. Consequently, forest and natural resources loss index, presence of 'hot spots' and mega-diversity in the state are serious concern of the day. Under unrelenting population pressure, subsistence farmers have stripped forest cover from the hill terrain of the State. The poor and underprivileged highlanders are the most visible agents of destruction in degraded environments. Poor highlanders depend heavily on natural resources for direct income and their poverty offers them few choices. There is no alternative planning that the underprivileged groups of highlanders could switch on for sustainable growth by generating income from their natural surroundings. Here and elsewhere, the poor stand at the end of a long chain of cause and effect. They are the messengers of un-sustainability rather than its agent. Therefore, it is of acute need to modernize the Jhumming practices so these poor highlanders are able to enjoy life with meaningful participation in the developmental planning.

(B) Resources of the Valley Region

Geographically, the State is located in a zone where the world's heaviest rainfall is recorded. Currently the State receives 142 cm rainfall annually. More than 60 per cent of the annual rainwater was received during four months i.e. June to September only. Because of various environmental problems the people of both hills and valley face the problem of drought in the lean season while occurring floods during the monsoon. It is also worth mentioning here that there were about 500 lakes and wetlands all through the interfluves region of the Manipur Valley river system. The existence of large number of lakes and wetlands in the valley itself is a unique ecosystem of the world. These wetlands support high levels of biological diversity in the valley of Manipur. They also offer sanctuary to a wide variety of plants, invertebrates, fishes, amphibians, reptiles and mammals, as well as thousands of both migratory and sedentary water birds. These valley wetlands are not only sites of exceptional and contemporary societies. Since ancient times, valley dwellers have lived along watercourses, benefiting from wide range of goods and services available from wetlands. Valley wetlands are an integral part of the hydrological cycle of the State, playing a key role in the provision and maintenance of water quality and quantity as the basis of all life in this State. They are often interconnected with other terrestrial ecosystems, mountain and degraded of all ecological systems. Till today wetlands are commonly regarded by planners and authorities' concerned as unproductive, unhealthy land. Very often government supporters and backing parties have made considerable efforts to encroach upon the wetlands to reclaim and convert them from a natural system to agricultural partitions and fisheries buns and ponds were constructed inside the wetland areas. Many have been filled with domestic, agricultural and urban wastes (some of which have been of toxic nature), while others have been drained to create additional land for the so-called development.

In the past 50 years, the rate of wetland loss has increased dramatically, and is still continuing. Special mention needs to be made here of the Loktak Lake, the biggest freshwater lake in the northeastern India that since the last couple of decades it has been consistently shrinking. Within the last two decades, 30 per cent of the natural water area of the Loktak Lake has already shrunk. Despite huge investment of money in Loktak Multipurpose Project, the average projected land to be brought under irrigation is marginal and power generation has not proved to be profitable in the context of year long power failure and load-shedding in the State. The project poses a threat to the people and environment of the State and people in the peripheral villages in particular. The negative impact of the degradation of Loktak Lake is clearly discernible from the predicament of the fishing community. For the normal functioning of Loktak Hydro Electric Project, the water level of the lake has to be maintained at a particular high level throughout the year. Consequently, it has created serious difficulty and misery for fishing community. At one stroke, they have been deprived of their traditional techniques of fishing. Considering the above-mentioned facts we need a detail survey particularly of land resources of the State. Today, land uses survey and land resource potential classification can be done so accurately by applying remote sensing devices. After the survey and classification planners may work development planning totally based on its natural resources.

Sustainable Development Planning

It is also well aware that any kind of developmental planning or establishment of industries, which does not based on its local specific resource, Manipur could not compete with the technique and application of multi-million companies. Subsequently the world's trends of development activities are always influenced by the activities of privatization, globalization/liberalization and also information technology. Therefore, considering the current trend the only viable development approach in Manipur may be of endemic in nature and ethnic character based development may be formulated. Prevailing geographic location and corresponding natural resources and cultural reflection of the people of Manipur may favour for formulation of plant-based drug and pharmaceutical product industry and tissue culture products. In this process each and every individual community may apply their indigenous knowledge system with the intervention of modern science and technological approaches. In order to achieve the main goal of sustainable development, the State needs to establish biotechnological institute so that the people of the State may be empowered for exploring the bio-resources.

Secondly, considering varied topographical features and its corresponding micro-climatic conditions which exhibit varieties of scenic resort stations is naturally located in almost all places of the State of Manipur. These scenic resorts are the gift of the nature to its people. Hence people of Manipur shall have the capacity to explore the resources of resort heritages for the benefit of the people. In this context, we may consider Tourism as one of the most appropriate industries where multiple and all walks of life is able to catelite activities of sustainability. It may also be considered as the only industry where the machine and computer could not replace the activities of human beings. It is the only industry where all walks of lives and different culture and endemic heritages harmoniously cherish the social and cultural values along with the developmental involvement. Considering the inner value and spirit of humanity, tourism industry is the only means for sustainable development basically based on its natural resources. The different multi ethnic communities in the hills of Manipur and their traditional way of life, art and crafts, weaving and their monolith culture are of high value in the present day trend of resource mobilization. Over and above, there are varieties of natural locations where the nature attract people of eco-tourism. Some of them may be mentioned here as follows – Dzuku Valley, Khyang, Siroi Peak, Mt. Esso, Kharasom Booning, Kailam, Barak Waterfalls, Zeilet Lake, Lokchao, Tharaon Cave, Khamkhui Cave, Rani Caves, Loktak and other wetlands, all the river systems are of high potential for adventure and water sports under the activities of eco-tourism. However, to activate this development process the planner needs to have a detail exercise for mapping the compact resource potential for linking by a well infrastructural development. Once tourism could cope up with as an industry the sustainable development could be achieved. For effective and meaningful participation in this section the people of Manipur should be empowered by giving appropriate education and training within a stipulated time.

Thirdly, the choices of sustainable planning basically need to choose resources that are generally endemic in character i.e. not common to other states and countries of the world. As for example, developmental strategies should be based on Natural heritage like Loktak Wetland/Lake, Bio-resources of the State, and cultural heritages of the people of the State etc.

1. Loktak Lake (A Ramsar Site) as natural heritage resources for sustainable development may be selected. Loktak Lake itself is a resourceful heritage for sustainable development, in terms of based on her water resources, its biomass locally known as *Phumdee*, its habitats, its fishes, its art and craft, its literature and as a climatic genome of the State.
2. These natural heritages may be grouped into three distinct subgroups viz. i) Water, ii) flora and fauna and iii) indigenous knowledge system and its aesthetic values. Based on water resources the Loktak Hydro Electric Project was commissioned as early as 1980. However, Lake Ecology and habitat systems were extremely degraded.

The power generation of course is owned by the National Hydro Electric Power Corporation (NHPC) but not by the State. Hence, this kind of development project is not directly benefiting its people rather the people are losing their natural heritage of Loktak. But still then the water area of the Loktak is feasible for water sporting, waterways in between the peripheral villages, harvesting of aquatic vegetable and fisheries etc. There are number of floating fishing huts locally called "Phumsang" used for their traditional fishing practices. These floating huts may be transformed into fishing hut cum tourist floating house with extension of minimum facilities. This may correlate with the introduction of canoeing or boating or rowing connectivity to the Phumsangs for visitors or local fish collectors. Currently, due to high eutrophication of lake water a vast and huge biomass was thickly growing in the lake. This creates serious problem of pollution deteriorating water quality and reducing the surface water area of the Lake. However, the Loktak Development Authority (LDA) is experimenting on this biomass by turning it into bio-fertilizer. If this kind of process is scientifically examined and test proves it will be of high value to the agriculture population of the State. Subsequently the State departments may have a coordinated composite planning, utilizing Loktak as a natural heritage for sustainable development in the region. This specific area based planning may choose eco-tourism industry a one of the most appropriate ones. However, there is need to establish well-defined and enforceable right (customary rights) and security of tenure, and ensuring of equal access to land, water and other natural and biological resources. Water governance arrangements should protect ecosystems and preserve or restore the ecological knowledge for a sustainable development of the area. It is also a fact that majority of population in the State being mainly dependent upon their natural resources linked land use activities for their livelihood concerned.

Conclusion

The long-term impact of industrialization, urbanization, exploitation and environmental degradation cannot be wished away. The problems are complex and choices of alternatives are difficult. Poverty and degraded environment are closely interrelated, especially in a State like Manipur where people depend for their livelihoods primarily on natural resource base of their immediate environment. Restoring natural resource systems and improving natural resource, management practices are a must for allowing grassroots peoples; empowerment and participation in the development strategies of the state. An environmental perspective must guide the evaluation of all development projects, recognizing the role of natural resources in the local and State level livelihoods. This recognition must be informed by comprehensive understanding of perceptions and opinions of indigenous people about their stakes in the natural resource based sustainable development planning.

Biomass is, and will continue as a main source of fuel and energy for the common people of the State. Realizing the fact, appropriate technology must be evolved for economy of biomass consumption efficiency of energy use, progressively less pressure on forest and green belt and less pollution etc.

The age-old traditional approaches to natural resource management such as sacred groves and ponds hills, water harvesting and traditional land use practices etc. should be revived by creating institutional mechanism which recaptures the ecological wisdom and spirit of community management inherent in those systems. Hence our common future for sustainable development can only be achieved with a better understanding of our common concerns and share responsibilities.

Further, it is also revealed that the developmental projects are prepared and imposed from outside or above not from below who needed them for their improvement. The people particularly the underprivileged are regarded as just objects and not subjects of development. Projects are not undertaken for the benefit of people but people are used for projects for the benefit of the affordable groups. All these factors are accentuating the existing disparities in between the hills and valley and the urban and rural etc.

Therefore, the sustainable development calls for multi-faceted and comprehensive intervention to address wide varieties of problems of the people and the State. The community, for whom the development programmes are meant, must take part in planning execution.

REFERENCES

1. Government of India, *Economic Survey 1999-2000,* New Delhi. Government of India, Ministry of Finance, 2000.
2. *Approach Paper to the Tenth Five Year Plan, 2002-2007,* New Delhi, Planning Commission, 2001.
3. S. Paul, "Community Participation in Development Projects: The World Bank Experience", *Readings in Community Participation,* The World Bank, Washington DC, 1987.
4. Uma Lake, *The Design for Rural Development: Lesson for Africa,* Baltimore, and John Hopkins, 1975.
5. M.L. Santhanam, " Human and Social Factors in Participation", *Journal of Rural Development,* Vol. No. 5, 1982.
6. Ch. Bala Ramulu, "Participatory Development: The Experience of Andhra Pradesh", *The Indian Journal of Public Administration,* Vol. XLVII, No. 4, 2002.
7. R.K. Ranjan Singh & H. Priyokumar Sharma, *Wetlands of Manipur,* Vol. I, Manipur Association for Science and Society, Integration House, Palace Compound, Imphal, 1999.
8. R.K. Ranjan Singh, "Land Potential Classification of the Manipur Valley". *Manipur University Research Journal,* Vol. III No. 1, Canchipur, Imphal, 1986.
9. ----------, *Global Environmental Concerns,* New Delhi, 2000.
10. Kaka D. Iralu, "Is Underdevelopment the Cause of Insurgency in Nagaland ?," *Dimensions of Development in Nagaland,* Indian Council of Social Science Research-North-Eastern Regional Centre, Shillong, 2002.
11. Govt. of India, *Economic Survey 1999-2000,* New Delhi, Govt. of India, Ministry of Finance, 2000.
12. *Approach Paper to the Tenth Five Year Plan,* 2002-2007, New Delhi, Planning Commission, 2001.
13. S. Paul, "Community Participation in Development Projects: The World Bank Experience", *Readings in Community Participation,* The World Bank, Washington DC, 1987.
14. Uma Lake, *The Design for Rural Development: Lesson for Africa,* Baltimore, and John Hopkins, 1975.
15. M.L. Santhanam, "Human and Social Factors in Participation", *Journal of Rural Development,* Vo. No. 5, 1982.

16. Ch. Bala Ramulu, "Participatory Development: The Experience of Andhra Pradesh", *The Indian Journal of Public Administration,* Vol. XLVII No. 4, 2002.

17. R.K. Ranjan Singh, "Land Potential Classification of the Manipur Valley", *Manipur University Research Journal,* Vol. III No. 1, Canchipur, Imphal, 1986.

18. R.K. Ranjan Singh & H. Priyokumar Sharma, *Wetlands of Manipur,* Vol. I, Manipur Association for Science and Society, Integration House, Palace Compound, Imphal, 1999.

19. ------------, *Global Environmental Concerns,* New Delhi, 2000.

20. Kaka D. Iralu, "Is Underdevelopment the Cause of Insurgency in Nagaland ?", *Dimensions of Development in Nagaland,* Indian Council of Social Science Research-North-Eastern Regional Centre, Shillong, 2002.

14

Heritage Tourism in Manipur: Problems and Prospects

Introduction

Legacy from the past – what we live with today and what we pass on to the future generations may be termed as *heritage, natural and cultural* heritages are the main sources of life, inspiration and identity of a region and its inhabitants. Natural heritages are endemic as well as unique to the region only. The natural heritages are the main catalysis in modelling and shaping of cultural heritages of the indigenous communities of a region. However, there are many atochthonous cultural elements influencing and adopting as one of the cultural heritages in the region.

Any place or region on the globe is endowed with its natural and cultural heritage, with its pride and privilege of the inhabitants of the area. Manipur is one of the uniques in natural and cultural resources among the diversified cultural and natural heritages of Indian Union. The existence of its distinct cultural flavours with bountiful natural resources is the essence of heritage tourism in Manipur. This is the basis of life and livelihood of the local communities. And these are the very same resources that the tourists came to enjoy and experience.

Further, tourism deals with attitudes and psyches, much like media and advertising. It is an industry that is involved in selling experiences, and not just tangible products.

The tourist is willing to pay not just for a place that is seen, or services that are rendered, but an entire package of experiences. Thus, tourism has the *Columbus attitude* as a cornerstone, whereby the experience of being an explorer, or of being the first in an undiscovered destination, which are carefully retained in their *'original state'*, mostly in pockets, in order to cater to the ever changing demand for new and different experiences. Tourism also involves influencing people to visit destinations, dealing therefore with the entire ambit of human motivations, likes and desires.

Tourism as an industry is a whole package of services, which will cease to exist if it is not for the natural heritage (resource) rich, culturally diverse countries or regions/ State, which can be showcased at a price, for the experience and comfort. Thus, tourism may be projected as a harbinger of investment, and consequently development while being an environment and indigenous people friendly activities. The problems and prospects of heritage tourism in Manipur may be focused as follows:

Manipur

"Imphal: A Flower on Lofty Heights" ?

(Takane no Hana – A Japanese Proverb)

'A Paradise on the Earth' ?

'A Jewel of India' ?

These are some of the paraphrases describing the natural and cultural heritages of the state of Manipur. The erstwhile royal state of Manipur is located at the geo-cultural tri-juncture of the Indo-Malayasian and Tibeto-Mongoloid sub-Himalayan phenomenon. One of the oldest states in the North East India, Manipur enjoys its own distinctive identity with vigorous enthusiasm. The State covers an area of about 22,390 sq. km. stretching in between the reticules of 92058'33.7"E to 94°44'53.0"E longitude and 23°50'05.40"N to 25°42'28.5"N latitude. The total perimeter of the State is 953 km (Burma) in the east and south. The average elevation of the State is ranging from 20 m above mean sea level to 2994 m above mean sea level.

Topographically, 80 per cent of the state's total area is mainly hilly/mountainous zone while the rest 20 per cent may be treated as river valley region. The hydrological regime of the state is controlled by the world's two great drainage basins i.e. the Brahmaputra – Barak basin and the Irrawaddy-Chindwin basin. The western hilly terrain region of the state is drained by the first basin system while the eastern portion including the *valley of Manipur* is drained by the second system of drainage basin.

The valley of Manipur is drained by the main tributaries of the Manipur River. The head streams of the Manipur River are the Iril, the Imphal, the Thoubal, the Chakpi, the Khuga, and the Nambool etc. In between the interfluves of these tributaries, there are a number of wetlands and lakes. Among them the *Loktak*, the biggest fresh water lake of the North East India, is located in the south western corner of the Manipur Valley. This lake or wetland is the only habited area of the *Brow Antler Deer*, popularly known as *'Sangai'* (the dancing deer), the rarest endanger species in the world.

The valley of Manipur is oval in shape and is surrounded by ranges of blue hills. It is the home of the *Meitei* who dominate the populace among other colourful communities. The serenity of these pristine and isolated environs influences the lifestyle of the inhabitants with a lavish hand, allowing them to live for centuries in harmony.

The entire hilly terrain region is inhabited by 33 different ethnic communities of highland. These ethnic highlanders were intermingled with hilly lore of forested dales, fountains, streams and waterfall etc. for many centuries and allow them to exhibit many varieties of distinct colourful ethno-culturally synthesized heritages. These hilly terrain mountain regions are the home of diversified bio-resources.

Problems

Considering the above mentioned basic facts, Manipur is one of the unexplored destinations of the tourists. Despite the existing resourcefulness of natural and cultural heritages in the state, tourism is not able to flourish as an economic activity in the state. Whereas, in some states, it creates income and employment opportunities, particularly in remote and backward areas, strengthens national integrity and promote international understanding by intensifying socio-cultural exchanges among people from different regions and countries. Here in this context the author of this paper is trying to identify the factors for retardation of tourism development in the state.

The first and foremost encounter is the mindset of the inhabitants and their inherent nature of the society. Common people, in general, are having a tendency of suspicious to the outsiders or visitors in the area. This kind of closeness in society was one of the defensive mechanisms for the survival of the society which is still acting as hangover to these days also. On the other hand, the state's culture is deeply rooted in a pluralistic ethos of age-old ethno history of the different indigenous communities providing creative expression, value-sustain and belief patterns to society. In order to explore the heritage tourism potentials in the state, capacity building and self empowerment of the common people is one of the utmost tasks of the policy makers of the state.

Secondly, the state is yet to make cataloguing as well as documenting all the spots and complexes of the natural heritages located at different places of the state. Further, varieties of distinct cultural events existing at different inhabited locations and inter-communities of the state have to be documented. After having all these information, a complete mapping, basic infrastructural facilities are to be extended. At present there is not enough standard service provider system. World class infrastructure would be created by improving the network of national and state highways and rural and inter village roads in and around the natural heritages and the heritage buildings. Over and above these tourist interest products and issues relating to price, security, health, safety and quality etc. would be studied.

Thirdly, more emphasis is given to preservation and protection of the archaeological and natural heritages, development of the monument complexes and museums. Further, efforts will have to be made to preserve and promote classical, folk and tribal art and crafts and oral traditions, which are in danger of extinction.

Lastly, the potential impact of climate change on the cultural and natural heritage is also a subject of growing concern. And hence, protection of natural and cultural heritage in order to create an appropriate framework for the preservation of our heritage for the benefit of current and future generations is a must. For this we may make awareness that our fragile ecological balance could be dramatically and irremediably disrupted as a consequence of certain unchecked human activities.

Prospects

Heritage tourism in Manipur offers ample scope to excel its natural and cultural resources, provided the above listed problems were properly addressed to at least at minimum level. The bitter prospects may ignite from the wondrous balance of flora and fauna that abound in its environment. Responding the rhythms of topographical features and micro-climate flavours, the state exhibit a combination of wet forests, temperate forests and pine forests that sustain a host of rare endemic plant and animal lives. This *Shangri-La* of natural wonders and cultural traditions are to be enjoyed at leisure. Home of colourful people and dazzling rituals, myth and legends, lively festivals and an evocative classical dance form, martial arts and indigenous games (Polo-Sagol Kangjei, Mukna

Kangei and Kang), Manipur may be able to attract diversity of tourists all the year round. Village tourism or community tourism at different community areas of both hills and plain may provide another aspect of heritage tourism involving the common people by empowering the participatory spirit in the community.

Eco-tourism is one of the brighter prospects of the State, which may include an integrated project on mountaineering and trekking in the hilly terrain, highlighting the grandeur of the highland communities. Subsequently, focus on jungles, ethnic people and heritage villages should be given. In this context, adventure tourism destination may be projected for the following villages along with the natural heritages namely *Willong, Yangkhuland, Mao Song Song, Mt. Esso and Dzuku valley, Purul Akutpa, Purul Atongba, Thangal Surung, Oinam, Hengbung of Senapati District; Khasom, Nungbee, Siroi Peak, Khamkhui Cave, Chatric, Lungpha, Khayangfall, Kochouphung Lake, Angoching of Ukhrul District; Kwatha, Lokchao Wild Life Sanctuary, Moreh, New Somdal, Sajik Tampak, Serou, Mombi, Chakpikarong of Chandel District; Thangjing Peak, Salangthel, Thanlong, Taipaimukh, Vihang, Kailam wildlife sanctuary of Churachandpur District; Barak Waterfall, Tharon Cave, Rani Cave, Zielet Lake, Bunning Tampak, Khoupum Waterfall of Tamenglong District*. Further it may also explore the hydrological regime of the state in terms of – water based adventure tourism like rafting to the Barak River etc. Considering the sites above with its pristine beauty and the surrounding magnificent terrain of unique flora and fauna holds potential as a significant *eco-tourism destination.*

Based upon the opportunity available in the state, and more specifically in the valley of Manipur (Imphal Battle Field of the Second World War), may harness the potentials of the Loktak Lake and its Keibul Lamjao National Park and surrounding hills and moles for the development of aquatic based nature tourism along with cultural and socio-cultural, arts and crafts promotion tourism.

Manipur is also favourable for the promotion of Cross-Border pilgrim tourism and golf tourism as well. In this context, the relaxation of the Restricted Area Permit and Inner Line Permit rules is needed as far as practicable. Such processes are the main "which is physical and psychological barrier to tourist and investor" (Sri Ved Prakash Marwah His Excellency the Governor of Manipur to the Manipur Legislative Assembly on 31-3-2000). A kind of liberalization is urgently needed to attract more international tourists.

After considering the gap between the problems and prospects, we can think of some action plan to minimize the gap. The author likes to highlight some points towards the action plan. The thrust would be given on IT based dissemination of information, joint campaigns through partnerships/sponsorships, gathering market intelligence and a brand building of state in India, with an aim to India's position distinctively on the Global map. Moreover, integrating Wild Life Sanctuaries and National Parks with tourism, promoting adventure/eco-tourism and bird watching etc. is urgently called for.

Tourism is a new development panacea for the North-eastern states of India and an important component of the government's ambitious plan for development of the country's North-eastern region. Financially too, central and state governments have been pouring funds into tourism development in the Northeast. No doubt, it is the scenic beauty, rich cultural heritage and historical importance of the region along with its relatively low accessibility in the past, which has led to its being highlighted as the *'unexplored'* tourist destination. Promotional material on NE tourism issued by the Ministry of Tourism describes the region in the following words: "The colourful tribal costumes and handicrafts, the friendly folk, coupled with the endless diversity in geography, flora and fauna, languages, customs and architecture of the monasteries have begun to attract scores of people". The Look East Policy of the government of India and using tourism as a tool to integrate the North-eastern region with South-east Asia have also been emphasized by authors like Bezbaruah (2005).

Nowadays, Tourism is treated as the second largest industry all over the world. It is also considered as a 'smokeless industry'. However, the notion of 'sustainable tourism' are intrinsically rooted in the western concept of environmentalism that do not take into account basic livelihood needs of communities in the poor region and therefore cannot be treated to situations of chronic poverty, glaring income inequities and even conflict-prone zones. The unsuitability of mass tourism infrastructure projects can be explained with the example of Thailand, which is suffering the adverse impacts of large scale tourism. Eco-tourism has meant deforestation with vast tracts of contiguous forests being cleared for tourism-related infrastructure like highways, airports, hotels, resorts, golf courses, visitor centres and other facilities. Research also reveals that over the past two decades, Manipur have lost substantial forest cover due to logging, saw-milling, shifting cultivation and even anti-insurgency efforts. The plethora of infrastructure projects proposed for the state are bound to add to this deforestation and if not carefully implemented the proposed tourism activities may cause more adverse effects. Further it is also evident that economically the larger numbers does not always result in large incomes for local communities in tourism essentially because benefits do not trickle-down to the community-level. Tourism in Manipur is still at the state of initial inception. Hence, the state has a long way to go before it can encompass tourism as a successful industry in the State.

15

Development of Transport and Communication System in the Hill Districts of Manipur

Geo-economic Background

Development processes and progress of a country or State basically depend upon the Geo-economic background of the area. However, the degree of development of an area also depends upon the resources, the way of its utilization and ability of technical application to the resource mobilization. In order to achieve a systematic and sustainable resource utilization we need an appropriate infrastructural development. Among the infrastructures, transport and communication are of prime importance. Manipur State is one of the most backward States in the country. It is because of the fact that the minimum requirements of transport and communication facilities are not yet attended to in the State. As a result, almost the whole of the State and more specifically Hill districts are the worst affected areas. Taking advantages of lack of communication facilities and resultant isolation and under-education, the ignorant common tribal people are often dependent on a few local elites, insincere politicians and exploiters. Lack of means to win greater access to resources and markets and to prevent the imposition of unworkable programme or technologies the common tribal people suffer extremely. The lesson is clear: unless the common highlanders are given the means to participate fully in the developmental works, they will continue to be excluded from its benefits. This should be realized and provoke a new alternative developmental concept for maximum extension of transport and communication system in the hilly areas of the State. The basic fault in the past developmental approaches in the State is that the ignorant common hill people are rarely consulted in the developmental planning and usually they have no role in the development activities. That is why the vast majority of the poor and ignorant have no time to represent their interest. Recent years have shown growing criticism of hill development strategies and efforts that have failed to deliver goods on their promises. These conventional strategies have been developed primarily as a series of technical transfers aimed at boosting and generating wealth for the elite groups and insincere politicians only. Even the basic and primary essential commodities and services do not reach the people of the region. Hence, common grass root people in the Hills are reduced to an alarming de-humanizing situation. In order to document the realities of the field situation, the author is trying to focus this paper on the following issues.

Geographically Manipur is a land of mountains dotted with inter-mountain valleys and wetlands. It has a total geographical area of about 22,327 sq. km. which constitutes less than 0.7% of the entire country. It lies in between the reticules of 23.8°N to 25.7°N and 93.5°E to 94.8°E with an average elevation ranging from 125 m.a.s.l. to 3000 m.a.s.l. It has a boundary line bordering with Myanmar in the East and South-east. The remaining 502 km of boundary line demarcated the State from other sister states like Nagaland to the North, Barak Valley of Assam in the west and Mizoram to the south-west.

The State also belongs to the same geological characters of the entire north-eastern region except in the case of Meghalaya plateau. In the early geological history the region experienced a massive movement of the Tethys Sea floor. This resulted in the upward and downward folding of the rocks. Characteristic features such as highland, ridges, basins and valleys were thus produced. All these topographic regions are susceptible to any of the seismic activities as the rock formation of this area is basically weak and unstable. A number of fault and thrust lines are recorded in most of the stream channels and major drainage system of the State in the north-south direction and also across the river basin etc. Over and above the stratigraphic characteristics of the rock pose a serious hurdle for undertaking major engineering and construction like mega dams, etc.

Ninety per cent (20,089 sq. km.) of the State's total area falls under the region of the hilly terrain and belongs to the five hill districts of the State. The Hill districts comprise of Chandel, Churachandpur, Senapati, Tamenglong and Ukhrul. The density of population is of 32 persons per square kilometer in the hills mostly dominated by the 29 tribes and sub-tribes of 1733 villages.

Although the State is one of the most backward ones in the country, the situation is more aggravated in the hilly region. There is no symptom of infrastructural developmental planning specifically in the hills and for common highlanders. Till now there is no scientific attempt to modernize the Jhumming cultivation system on which more than 80% of the hilly people depend upon for their livelihood. Further it is also a known fact that there are varieties of natural resources which could boost-up the economy of the hilly terrain inhabitants. All the flora and fauna and natural beauty are of priceless gift of nature to the indigenous population of the region and are of high value in the present trend of self-sustainable economy. Their habitats are richly endowed with natural resources (which however are being steadily depleted). The real potentialities of this region could be transformed into appropriate action only when the transport and communication network is made available. Otherwise, it is ironic that tribal people must live in poverty in the midst of plenty.

Current Status of Total Surface Road in the Hills

Every level of civilization and composite culture gained by the Manipuris are all passes through this hilly terrain. Manipur has been evolved with her 2000 years old history and traditions and exposed to outside world only through these terrains. But, unfortunately the light and wave of civilization is yet to reach in this region. Some of the historic routes are of great value to be mentioned herewith i.e. Nongpok Haram, Nongchup Haram, Tongjei Maril (Old Cachar Road), Heirok Lambee etc. the colour of Manipur civilization is flowing through these network but not even a single mode of culture is protected till today. On the other hand, their simple trusting nature has made them prey to ruthless exploitation at the hands of middlemen who collect forest produce and other items from the tribes at the pittance. All plan funds sanctioned for the development of the hill districts and the people were missing in the pockets of a few men like contractors and insincere leaders of the area. Common tribal people faced with hunger and poverty, they invariably find themselves in the clutches of the exploiters ending up in the vicious circle of bondage from which there is no reprieve. Government efforts towards tribal development have failed to achieve the expected results, despite the heavy allocation of funds for this purpose. The top heavy bureaucratic approach devoid of any community participation did not address their real needs as perceived by the indigenous highlanders of the State. Post independent development plan for linking inter-district and village roads were constructed and maintained only on paper. A huge amount had already been spent for inter- village roads under tribal welfare scheme that were also only in blue print but not even a single bridle pet were constructed properly. These are all clearly visible from the plan record and expenditure statement of the State.

As per records available from the State Government the total length of surface roads was 4,279 km in 1978. These include National Highways, State Highways, and District Roads. Based on the above mentioned information, the road density (in terms of length per unit area) and availability (length per unit population) is furnished hereunder.

TABLE 2

Road Density and Availability in the Hill Districts of Manipur

No.	*Region*	*Total Population*	*Area (sq. km.)*	*Total Length (km)*	*Road Density (km/ 1000 sq. km)*	*Road Availability (km/ 1000 persons)*
I	II	III	IV	V	VI	VII
1.	Manipur	1,420.953	22,327	8,646	387	6.09
2.	Hill Districts	491,876	20,089	5,728	285	11.65

The road density of the state at 387 km/1000 sq. km. compares fairly well with similar figures for other states of NE Region, i.e. Nagaland 300 km, Assam 290 km and Tripura 410 km. However, the National figure (1992) is 628.

The National Highways NH-39, NH-53 and NH-150 are the only lifelines of the State. NH-39 links with Dimapur of Nagaland and Tamu of Myanmar. NH-53 travels west from Imphal connecting with Cachar District of Assam via Tamenglong District and NH-150 with Jeshami Ukhrul via Imphal Churachandpur to Mizoram. The State has 527 km of State Highways connecting districts and Sub-Divisional Headquarters with Imphal, the capital city. Major District Roads connecting Sub-Divisional Headquarters to the District Headquarters and other important growth centres comprised a length of 466 km only. There is no air communication system in between the State capital and

District Headquarters except some helipads for defence purposes.

As per finding of the strategic option study of Manipur State Roads (Span Consultants Pvt. Limited – 2000) the busiest route is the State Highway connecting Imphal with Singhat via Bishnupur, Moirang and Churachandpur. Second busiest is NH-39 connecting Imphal with Moreh via Thoubal and Palel. Third is NH-39 from Imphal upto Tadubi and Mao, the highest traffic volume occurring on the section Imphal-Karong-Senapati. Imphal city is the focal point for all the major roads and it acts as a CBD area of the State as a whole.

TABLE 3

District-wise Road Density – 1994

	District	*Area (sq. km.)*	*Road Length (km)*	*Road Density*
A. Valley Districts				
i) & ii)	Imphal (East & West)	1,228	1,760	1,425
iii)	Bishnupur	496	443	894
iv)	Thoubal	514	726	1,412
	Valley Total	2,238	2,929	3,731
B. Hill Districts				
i)	Senapati	3,271	1,154	353
ii)	Ukhrul	4,544	1,827	402
iii)	Chandel	3,313	688	208
iv)	Churachandpur	4,570	1,028	224
v)	Tamenglong	4,391	1,035	236
	Hill Total	**20,089**	**5,732**	**1,423**
	Manipur	**22,327**	**8,646**	**387**
	All India (1992)	**3,287,263**	**2,065,039**	**628**

Source: Basic Road Statistics, Manipur, 1997 & Census of India, 1991.

All the existing surface road network as well as vehicular volume and alignments are traditionally controlled by the physio-topographic distinctions between the flat central valley and the surrounding hill areas. Further, the elongated and narrow shape of the central Manipur valley region has influenced the transportation network to make north-south-alignments. As a result District wise road density is far behind the State as well as the National density.

The table 3 clearly shows the relative road infrastructure development in the State. The low density of roads in the State is accounted mainly of low density of roads in the Hill Districts of Manipur. The density of roads in the hill districts range from as low as 136 km/1000 sq. km in Chandel to 282 km/1000 sq. km in Ukhrul. Therefore, priority on road development strategy should be made by emphasizing the necessity of low density in hill districts of Manipur. Such kind of approach may lead to a successful sustainable development in the State. This may act as a catalyst for emergence of horticulture and spice based activities and eco-tourism policy matter the road networking should be planned connecting all the focal growth points and sub-divisional headquarters and district headquarters to the capital city of Imphal. Secondly, based on the resource potential and free trade, the State should have extended the road network to the following growth potential areas.

A. Three Major Outer Ring Roads

1. Bishnupur, Khoupum, Nungba, Tamenglong, Motbung, Saikhul, Litan, Phungyar, Kashom Khullen, Thoubal and Bishnupur.
2. Churachandpur, Tharon, Phaijang, Keiphundai, Namtiram, Tamei, Tuyang, Kangpokpi, Chongla, Tuinem, Ukhrul, Shansak Khullen, Kamjong, Kashom Khullen, Gomi, Tengnoupal, Chakpi Karong, Sugnu to Churachandpur.
3. Singhat, Bukpi, Hanship, Parbung, Tipaimukh,

Jiribam, Tousem, Katang, Magulong, New Khunpung, Kulong Naga, Yangkhulen, Maram, Tadubi, Lai, Jessami, Wahong, New Tusom, Challo, Ching-Ngai, Chammu, Choro Khunou, Kangpat Khullen, Kwatha, Moreh, Yangoulen, Molcham, New Somtal, Sajiktampak to Singhat.

B. New Corridor Roads

(i) Kangpokpi, Tousem to Jowai via. Nagaland.

(ii) Ukhrul, Jessami to Phek.

(iii) Heirok, Sita, Soibol, Yangoupokpi to Mintha (Myanmar).

(iv) Ukhrul, Chatric.

(v) Imphal-Diphu via. Eroisemba, Waichong, Tamenglong, four District of Nagaland to Diphu of Karbi-Anglong, Assam.

(vi) Karong to Diphu.

(vii) Sugnu to Bokan (Myanmar) via. Jaupi, Yangoulen and Molcham etc.

Conclusion

In conclusion, one can easily deduce from the district-wise road density figures stated earlier that the kind of transport bottlenecks being faced in the hilly areas. Superimpose these conditions on the difficult terrain of the hills and the problem is extremely enormous. This makes the hill economy a much more costly and serves as a double constraint on development. As there is low level of economic activity in the hills, real wages are low there and due to higher transport costs, prices are higher. Therefore, while considering the issue of prioritizing the development of road transport and communication system in the Hills of Manipur, the level of connectivity in between the Districts, districts to sub-divisional headquarters, sub-divisional headquarters to villages, inter-villages and to the State capital has to be increased and should be made available for the places and people of the region.

It should also aim at raising of production system of the area, increasing accessibility to facilities and governance, and increasing socio-physical interactions etc. This may create a congenial atmosphere for the integrity of the whole of the State.

Lastly, development of road transport and communication network system in the Hill Districts of Manipur should try to reduce the time and transportation cost of both people and commodities in order to reduce the cost of production while at the same time facilitating marketing setup, conservation of natural and cultural heritages of the region. Further it should also serve as a catalyst for emergence of new productive activities among the highlanders.

REFERENCES

1. Census of India, 1991. Directorate of Census Operation, Manipur-1998
   (a) Series – 15
   (b) Part-III – B Series
   (c) Part-IV – A-C Series
   (d) Part-II – A
   (e) District Census Hand Book – 1991
2. *Transport and Communication in North East Region,* 1988 NEC, Shillong.
3. *Strategic Option Study,* 2000, PWD, Govt. of Manipur.
4. Survey Documents of Field Studies conducted by Manipur Cultural Integration Conference (MCIC) and Manipur Association for Science and Society (MASS) 1975 to 2001 February.

16

Geographical Perspectives of Regionalism: An Observation of Regionalism in North Eastern India

Concept of Regionalism

Ours is a cultural world in the sense that there are countless numbers of groups that find confidence and guidance from the fact that they each have a separate sense of being, of distinctiveness, which is largely derived from and indeed can be summed up by what we call "culture." But ours is also a political world, with political "interference" having caused the earth to be partitioned in ways that often make no sense from a cultural perspective. Many groups of people are united, at one level of generalization, simply because the bounding of territory has forced them to belong to integrated systems, the principal political limits of which are represented by the international boundaries of states. The emotional bounds of a group to politico-territorial identities, is defined loosely as the nation-state. We live out our lives within politically defined territorial units, but much of our existence relates to territorial organizations that are far removed from the personal level and yet often influence us directly.

Gottman some time ago suggested that "the most stubborn facts" in relation to the political partitioning of the world "are those of the spirit, not those of the physical world" and that "one of the most stubborn facts of the spirit remains nationalist feeling—at different scales". What is mean by this? Is it possible to have sub-state nationalisms as well as state nationalism? Perhaps we need to define our term further.

Cobban said of nation that "any territorial community, the members of which are conscious of themselves as members of the community, and wish to maintain the identity of their community, is nation". However, there is need to tie such notion of group identity to the concept of nationalism.

Shafer (1980), in defining nationalism, listed a series of sentiments that bound people and place, while Kedourie (1960) saw nationalism as a doctrine of pretense. Both scholars would agree that nationalism involve myth that relate to and encourage feelings of loyalty to and identification with a group's consciousness of itself and cause the group either to have or desire political independence under its own government in its own territory.

Interestingly, nationalism also demands the shifting of loyalties from local and regional groups to the nation, so organizations at suprastate levels also demand a shifting of loyalties. Under such circumstances the idea of region and regionalism has been emerged. Regionalism is the idea or practice of dividing a country/ nation into smaller units for political, economic, social and cultural purposes. Politically, regionalism is linked to decentralize or federalist government. Regionalism is both cultural and political, as its political success is linked to the development of a regional culture.

Gamble and Payne (1996) identified *regionalism* as 'a state-led or states-led project designed to recognize a particular regional space along defined economic and political lines'. Hveem (2000) defined *regionalism* as 'the body of ideas promoting an identified geographical or social space as the regional project'. This definition of regionalism reflects three important points: it focuses on a particular geographical area, it involves a regional project that pursues particular objectives, and it implies the creation of institution. In this sense, regionalism is both a political strategy aimed at certain objectives and the mechanism for achieving those objectives (Spindier 2002).

There is a wealth of theories on why regionalism arises, the circumstances under which it becomes popular, and what popular regionalism may bring in terms of political stability and economic development. Regionalism has, for instance, been defined as the attempt to safeguard regional culture, language or identity. Regionalism has also been understood as a political aspiration for 'far-reaching autonomy' at the regional level, or as the advocacy of geographical closeness between the citizens and their elected representatives. In other context, regionalism has been equated with sub-national movements striving for some type of autonomy or self-government within or outside the traditional state. In yet another cases, regionalism has been confused with regional consciousness, or described as something that by necessity develops within an ethnic community or from a sense of regional identity. Thus the main objective, therefore, is to give a comprehensive overview on different applications of the concept of regionalism in various social science disciplines, and in various empirical contexts. Therefore, regionalism has been topic of political science, regional planning studies, human, economic and political geography and will thus have an interdisciplinary.

Emerging Trend

The dramatic surge in regional cooperation schemes in the post-1980 period has been one of the most important developments in world politics. Significantly, countries like the United States, Canada, Japan, and China, which showed little interests in regionalism in the post-World War II period, have embraced regionalism with considerable enthusiasm in the post-Cold War era. What accounts for this recent spurt in regionalism? At least four developments seem to have come together in the late 1980s to create a momentum towards regionalism: expansion of European integration; the demise of Soviet Union; the shift in US strategy; and changing perspectives on regional trade and foreign investment in the developing world. South Asia is no exception to such worldwide trends. After more than eight years of negotiation, seven South Asian countries – Bangladesh, Bhutan, India, Maldives, Nepal, Pakistan, and Sri Lanka – come together in December 1985 to form the South Asian Association of Regional Cooperation (SAARC).

The map of India would be a patchwork of region, numbering probably more than ten but less than fifty, defined according to biophysical features, primarily watersheds, modified to recognize human settlement, local government boundaries and land use patterns.

Northeast India

Whether, the concept of regionalism is applicable to Northeast India as a separate entity in the larger context of the present trend of Regionalism. The degree of commonality among the diversified ethnicity of the Northeast India is yet to be defined urgently. However, the growth of a regional concept among the states of the Northeast India called for an ideology of pragmatic anti dependency which seeks to promote regional interdependency among the states of the region without delinking them from the national and the global system. The region aspire to achieve " structural empowerment" and, thus, hope to reduce the degree of dependence on the fund and manpower from the centre and act at the same time increase the collective bargaining in the national and global economy.

1. Need of emergence of common culture addressing needs and interest

2. NEC and DONER need some kind of policy which could help in evolving a cellular regionalism among the states of the Northeast India. So that Northeast India may be able to contribute its share to the Indian National role in the Regional Cooperational approach.

REFERENCES

1. Gamble, A. and Payne, A.(Ed) *Regionalism and World Order,* Basingstoke: Macmillan, 1966.

2. Hveem,H. 'Explaining the regional phenomenon in an era of Globalization,' in Stubbs,R. and Underhill (Ed), *Political Economy and the Changing Global Order,* Oxford: Oxford University Press 2000, pp. 70-81.

3. Spinder, M. *New Regionalism and the Construction of Global order,* CSGR working papers No 93/02, Centre for the Study of Globalization and Regionalization, March-2002.

17

A Geo-Strategic Study of Indo-Myanmar Region

A geo-strategic study of the Indo-Myanmar region needs a detail analysis of the tactical relations in between the tri-nations namely India-China-Myanmar. The main objective of this paper is to study the vibrant geopolitical pulses throbbing along Myanmar's border. Myanmar shares common borders with five countries: Bangladesh 193 km, China 2,185 km, Laos 235 km, Thailand 1,800 km and India 1,463 km.India dominates Myanmar's western side just as China dominates its northern borders. Thailand borders the entire east of Myanmar except for a narrow strip that borders Laos. The location of Myanmar is one of the strategic land bridges of India, linking South and Southeast Asia. But at the same time the geostrategic location of Myanmar at the tri-junction of East Asia, Southeast Asia and South Asia is of critical significance in India. Obviously, China's security interest in Myanmar is to gain promising land access to Indian Ocean and the Andaman Sea. In terms of energy security, this has become increasingly important with China's growing dependence on imported oil.

Secondly, as a littoral of the Indian Ocean, Myanmar's strategic value further increases. Its 1,930 km long coastline dominates the eastern arch of the Bay of Bengal, leaning to the Malacca Strait. Myanmar provides China's landlocked Yunan Province the shortest land and sea access to South

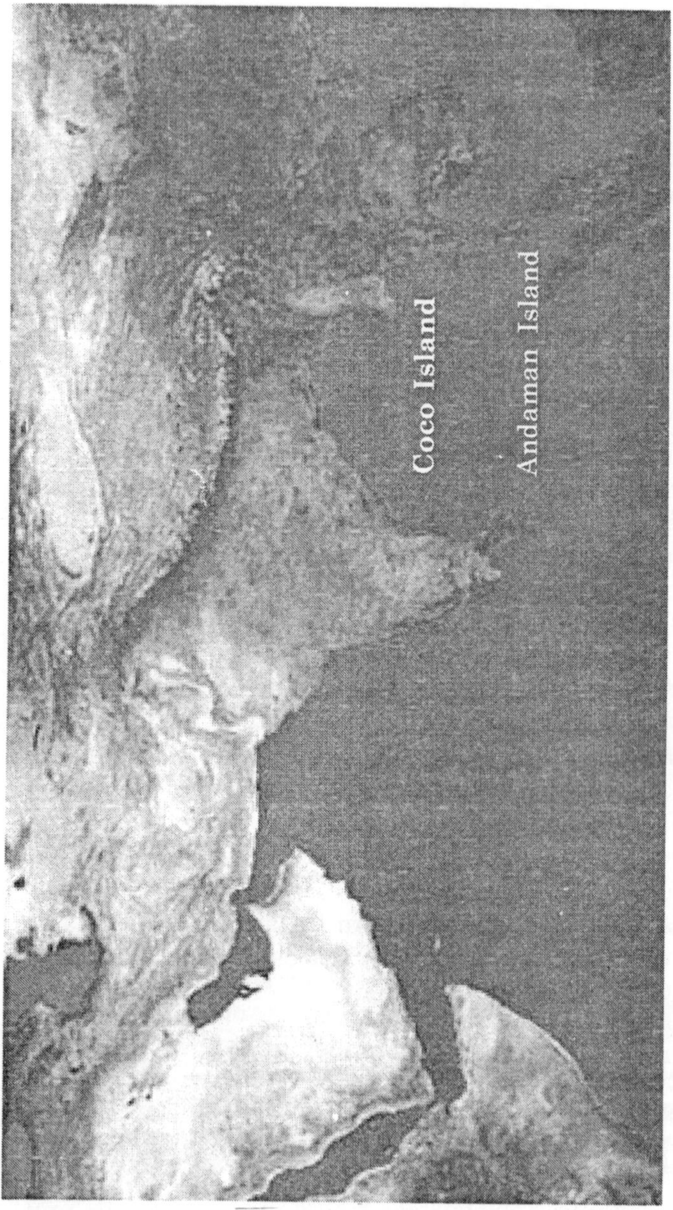
Coco Island
Andaman Island

Asia, just as it provides convenient external land and sea communication option to India's landlocked north eastern states. The oceanic boundaries of Myanmar are extremely concerned with maritime security of India, in particular the surrounding areas of the Coco Islands which is barely 30km away from the Andaman Islands. The setting up of a modern maritime reconnaissance and electronic intelligence system on the Great Coco Island by the Chinese is really a matter of serious concern for the Indian Ocean. This in conjunction with electronic surveillance facilities at the Alexandra Channel in the Andaman Sea, Indian military activities in Andaman Nicobar islands and the missile testing activities at Chandipore in Orissa can be monitored effectively by China.

Thirdly, both sides of the regions bordering Myanmar are mostly populated by ethnic communities with their own distinct ethnic, religious and linguistic identities from the rest of the country. However, the majority of Burmese populations, who are Buddhists, live in the fertile and more developed southern Myanmar with easier access from China. Thus, the northern ethnic regions have been neglected and remain underdeveloped. This caused the ethnic wars happening all along the Naga, Kachin and Chin areas bordering India. Similarly, the northeast India is a home of varied ethnic communities with different dialects and languages, indigenous belief and values of its own and ruled by different independent kingdoms before the establishment of the Union of India. Subsequently, many of the tribes in India's northeastern region are ethnically linked to the tribes on the Myanmar side of the border. Thus different kinds of ethnic militancy and war of independence have always affected the region.

Topographically the mountain ranges and rivers of Myanmar were running north-south direction. Therefore, construction of road communication and movement from India's north east with the same terrain feature to Myanmar are facing more hardship.

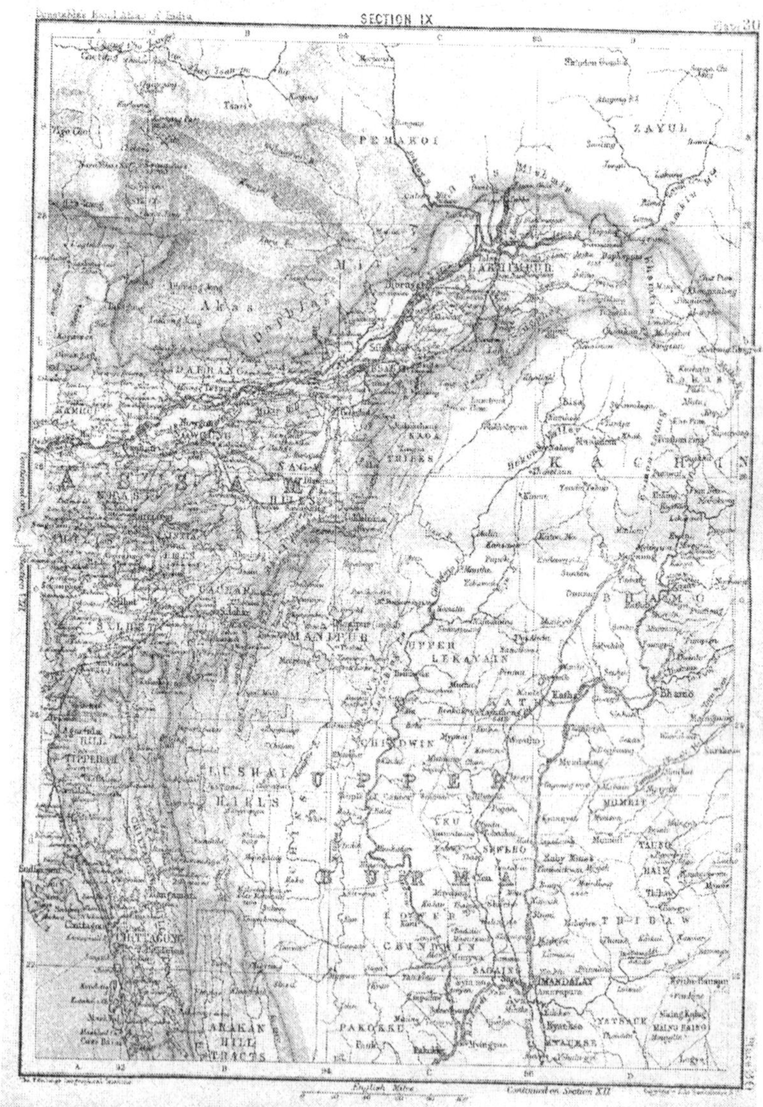

Source - Constable Atlas, 1893

At the same time it facilitates easier movement from Chinese border and provides for natural flow of communication. The Chinese have more favourable terrain configuration to build road from the Chinese border to Mandalay Division and up to the Ayeyarwaddy Delta. Further, Union of Myanmar provides the shortest access from Yunan Province of China towards India's eastern borders and these developments have special strategic signifance while India's northeastern states bordering Myanmar are not as well developed as Yunan province of China bordering Myanmar in the northeast. Thus, trade relation with China is faster than with India's northeastern region. Over the last two decades the Chinese have built very close economic, political, military and developmental relation with Myanmar. Further, the Chinese have used the geophysical advantage they enjoy to gain access to Myanmar's mineral and natural gas resources. Following a policy of **non-interference** in internal affairs of the country, China has become the main supplier of arms to Myanmar. Since 1980 China has been exclusively involved in Myanmar strategically and economically. Naturally the Government of India worried about the growing strategic links in between Sino-Myanmar. Currently, China has more leverage than India in seeking influence in Myanmar. There are more Chinese than Indian immigrants in the northern town of Myanmar, engaging in different kinds of trade and business. An estimation of the Chinese Embassy in Yangon revealed that there were more than two million Chinese in Myanmar in 2005, including half a million ethnic Chinese. In the cities of northern Myanmar, such as Mandalay, the influence of new Chinese migrants in almost all economic sectors is on the rise. These new Chinese immigrants have also become an important influence in Myanmar society. Over and above, China produces cheaper goods to sell than India.

Indo-Myanmar Relations

Considering all the viewpoints sighted above, the issues of Indo-Myanmar relationship shall have to be more pragmatic strategic approach while framing the national policies on external affairs. Further it is also necessary to look into the matters related with the population of about 3-4 lakhs of Indians who have settled there and the issues of territorial boundaries with the States like Manipur. The relationship between India and Myanmar were close during the first years after independence and during the formation of Non-Aligned Movement. Both countries signed a Treaty of Friendship, which was to remain in force "forever thereafter". Because of this Friendship Treaty the Kabow Valley was formally transferred to Myanmar which is against the interest of the people of Manipur. However, after the 1962 coup, relationship came to a standstill. India ignored its eastern neighbour due to the undemocratic regime that had taken over the assets of Indians living in Myanmar. After three decades i.e. from the early part of 1990 India's relationship with Myanmar began to recover. The restoration of relationship may be related with the growing concern and changing attitude of Myanmar from their traditional "strategic neutrality' policy to more tilting towards China. However, India's policy may try to remove Myanmar from China's orbit or sphere of influence.

India's strategic thinking may have greater cooperation with Myanmar on cross-border counter-insurgency efforts, building of pipeline for importing hydro-carbon resources from Myanmar through its northeastern region. The northeastern region is basically one of the most underdeveloped regions in the country and it may be the most effective way to neutralize the secessionist movements in the region.

Gas Pipe Line

But more importantly the geopolitical position of

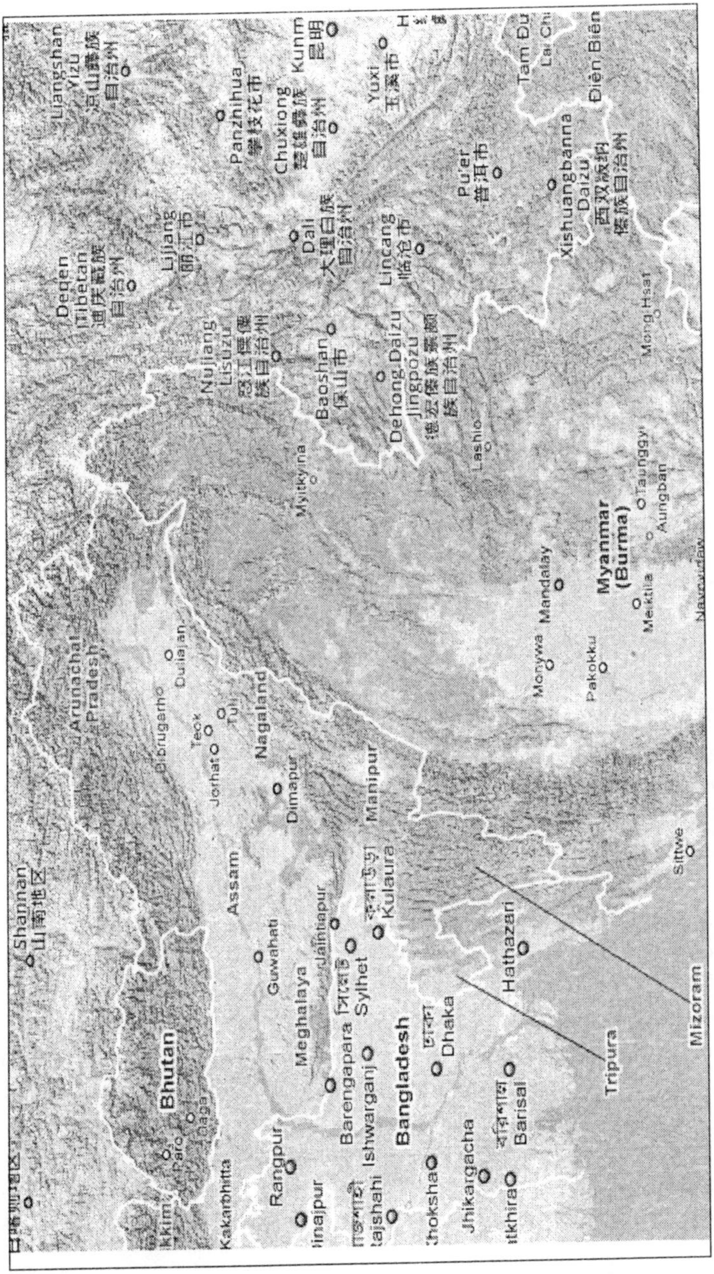

Proposed Gas Pipeline through Kabaw Valley

Myanmar in Southeast Asia is the key stepping stone in India's *Look-East Policy* which seeks to develop and expand political, economy and security ties with ASEAN. Thus, the North East India, the most remote part of the country may become the centre of development in the country. In the long term scenario, India may wish Myanmar become an independent market as well as the transit country and the link between South and Southeast Asia.

Given the geopolitical significance of Myanmar to both India and China, and the potential for rivalry between the two growing powers i.e. India and China, the Indian relation with Myanmar needs to examine the complex relation more specifically along the three dimensions viz. *Security, Energy and Economics.*

For the strategic Economic reasons, Myanmar's military junta has since the early 1990 pursued an "open-door" economic policy, embarking upon an ambitious programme of building roads, bridges, dams, hydroelectric schemes and import-substituting state-owned industries. Since 1988, China enjoys considerable share of benefit from Myanmar. Statistics showed that by 2005, China's total aid to Myanmar reached about US $ 100 million. After four years, in January 1994, India signed *Border Trade Agreement* with Myanmar and Implementated in April 1995, with the opening of a cross border point between Moreh (Manipur) and Tamu (Sagaing Division of Myanmar).However, economically, India started to engage Myanmar through sub-regional organisations like Bangladesh-India-Myanmar-Sri Lanka-Thailand economic cooperation (BIMSTEC) and the Mekong-Ganga Cooperation (MGC) which was founded in the later part of 2000. These projects underline cooperation in tourism, culture, education and language training; emphasize links between Indian traditional culture and Southeast Asian culture. Involvement in ASEAN infrastructural projects India will cooperate for extension of railway from New

Delhi to Hanoi, passing through Myanmar, Thailand, Laos and Cambodia and opening of new trade corridor in the Mekong sub-region. In order to make the involvement fruitful, India recently initiated a major project to link its isolated states of the northeastern region to Bay of Bengal via the Kaladan River and is investing in a new port in Sittwe. Further to improve connectivity with Myanmar, India has taken up a number of road and port construction projects. India has constructed the 160 km Tamu-Kalewa-Kalemyo road in Myanmar from Manipur border town Moreh. It is also assisting in the proposed Trans-Asian Highway project to connect Moreh in Manipur to Mae Sot in Thailand via Bagan in Myanmar. A proposal to construct a rail link from Jiribam in Manipur to Hanoi in Vietnam through Myanmar is also on the cards. Over and above, India is taking steps for extension of airlines with cooperation in areas like agriculture, telecommunications etc.

From the perspective of security, China and Myanmar have enhanced their military cooperation and exchange since 1988. The most significant move in this aspect was the 1990 deal involving weapons and military equipment worth an estimated US $ 1.2 billion; another agreement to supply weapons and equipment worth US $400 million in 1994. In 2003, China assisted Myanmar in building an 85-metre jetty to naval facilities on Great Coco Islands, which lies 18 km from Nicobar Island of India. Further, China has built a deep-sea port in Kyaukpyu in Rakhine state. Kyaukpyu is located on the route connecting southwestern China's Kunming city with Myanmar's Sittwe. It is also interesting to note that China has been a net oil importer since 1993 and rank second position among oil consumers after the US and accounted for 40% of the world's crude oil demand growth since 2000. Even then China is facing sporadic power shortages while growing car ownership and air travel across China and growing industries, agriculture, construction etc make more pressure on energy resources. As a result, energy security has become an area of vital importance to China's stability and security. Therefore, China is stepping up to control over the Indian Ocean maritime operation by investing in construction of ports at Gwadar in Pakistan, Arabian Sea coast, Chittagong port of Bangladesh and Colombo port etc. Considering the prevailing circumstances in and around the Indian Ocean and the insurgency in the North Eastern States of India, smuggling of arms, drug trafficking and narco-terrorism is the main security concern along the Indo-Myanmar border. The imbroglio of ethnic secessionism, religious and political insurgencies, large-scale smuggling and above all transnational links across border supports, have long undermined the relations between New Delhi and Yangon. Furthermore, courting the junta would also enable India to open up the North- East and in the long term crack down on all the smuggling in the region, particularly small and light arms proliferation, since Myanmar had become a well known trafficking corridor.

Energy Sector

Expecting an exponential growth in its energy demands due to expanding economy India has been trying hard in recent times to secure energy supplies. But unfortunately, India's oil diplomacy has not been sufficiently geared up to meet this challenge. As a result its oil companies have been outsmarted or rather outbidded by Chinese firms in several deals. Most embarrassingly, India has also lost a deal in Myanmar where no such bidding was held. This deal was lost purely because we could not respond properly to the prevailing situation in the subcontinent. India is planning to import gas from Iran, Myanmar and Turkmenistan via transnational gas pipelines to meet the growing energy needs, as domestic production is unable to meet its requirement. But the Union of Myanmar declined the gas supply to the Myanmar-Bangladesh- India pipeline. Instead, Yangon signed an agreement with Hong Kong-listed Petro

China, under which Myanmar's ministry of energy agreed to sell 6.5 TCF from Rakhine coastline reserve through an overland pipeline to Kunming (China) for 30 years. India has been eying huge hydrocarbon resources of Myanmar for quite some time. However, Myanmar decided to tie up with Chinese firm Petro China. It is definitely a setback to India's Oil diplomacy and its energy security. Considering the facts and circumstances of the prevailing geopolitics in the region, India will also have to integrate its Oil diplomacy with its foreign policy.

Conclusion

Since China is one of the most important players in Myanmar's domestic economy and foreign relations, Indian relationship with Myanmar must be established with a vision of close and practicable long-term relationship. As South- East Asia begins with Myanmar, the Indian diplomacy has to include Myanmar in its eastern diplomacy and could no longer isolate it as in the past. The Mekong-Ganga Cooperation (MGC) may strengthen the relationship among the common civilization background countries like Myanmar, Thailand, Cambodia, Vietnam and Laos for the riparian states of the Mekong River, and India for the Ganges River to counterbalance the Kunming Initiative of Mekong Basin Project. In this strategy, the Asian Development Bank (ADB) sponsored **Greater Mekong Sub Region** (GMS) project to integrate the economies of the countries like Thailand, China's Yunan Province and Myanmar. In this context more effort be made for the development of historic Indo-Burma roads to transform them into economic, diplomatic and business corridors linking India and the South-East Asia. Lastly, to have a better understanding and peaceful coexistence with Myanmar, India needs to resolve its border disputes with China and also to improve its relationship with neighbouring countries like Bangladesh, Sri Lanka and Pakistan. Resolving territorial disputes and reducing the ongoing uprising movements in the Northeastern region will become increasingly important for India if it is to fully exploit its proximity to a region on its eastern border.

REFERENCES

1. Poon Kim Shee, The Political Economy of China-Myanmar Relations: Strategic and Economic Dimensions, *Ritsumeikan Annual Review of International Studies,* Vol.1.pp33-53, The International Studies Association of Ritsumeikan University, Japan, 2002.

2. The South China Sea in China's Strategic Thinking, *Contemporary Southeast Asia,*Vol.19, No.4 March 1998, Singapore, p.369-387.

3. Zhao Hong, *China and India's Competitive Relation with Myanmar,* School of Southeast Asian Studies, Xiamen University.

4. Thin Thin Aung and Soe Myint, *India-Burma Relations* ,available at http://www.idea.in/asiapacific/burma/upload/chap4/pdf

5. Tarique Niazi, "Asia Between China and India", *Japan Focus,* May 31, 2006.

6. Erica Downs, Energy Security Series: China, The Brookings Foreign Policy Studies, December 2006. Available at: http: www.brookings.edu/fp/research/energy/2006china.htm

Index

Trapping and Killing of
Moorfalconat and migratory birds

Hunting and Killing of
State Bird (Nongeen)

Yangkhullen Chief's
House decorated with Trophies

Moorhen, Phubala

DZUKO Valley

Proposed Gas Pipeline
through Kabaw Valley

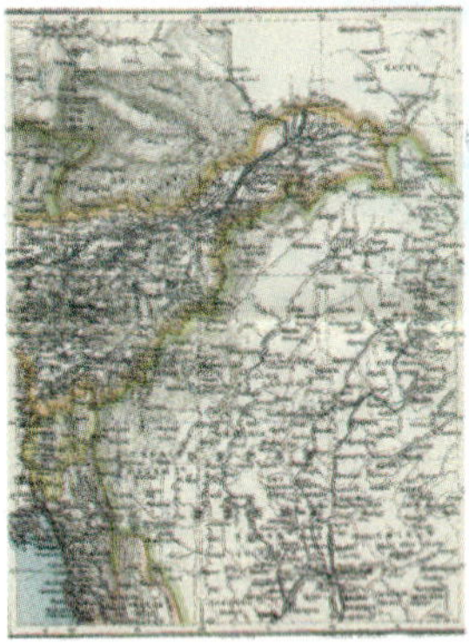

THD Dam Axis Site

Map Source
Down to Earth

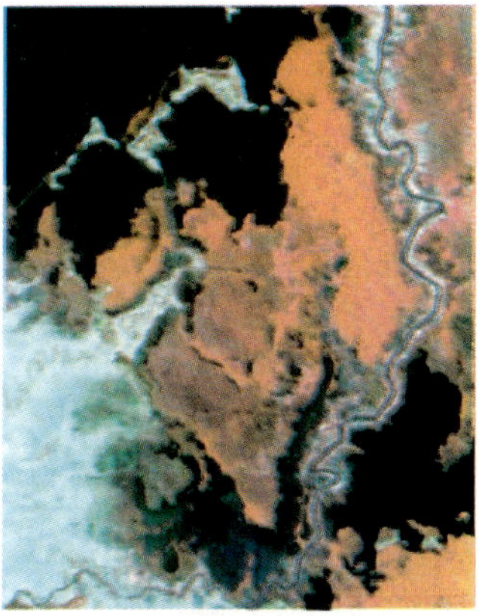

1989

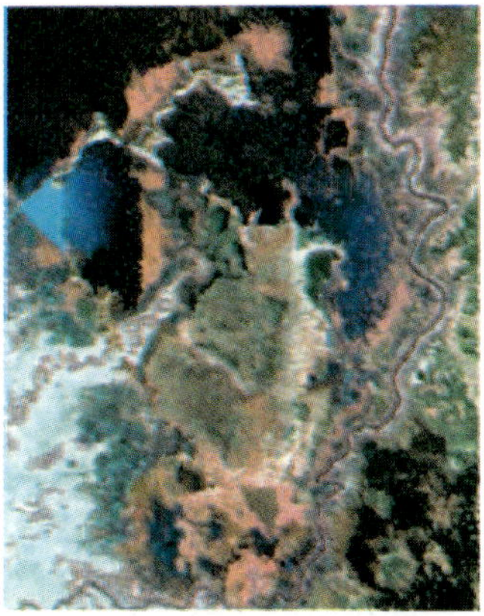

1999

2001

2002

Burned Hill slope for Jhuming